Microsoft®
Word for Office 365
Beginning
Instructor Guide

TABLE OF CONTENTS

DEVELOPMENT PHILOSOPHY

As an experienced instructor, you have probably taught from many training manuals, each developed/written in a different manner. Each developer has a distinct way of approaching a class and we are, of course, no different.

Our number one concern is to return control of the classroom to the instructor. Most of the training manuals written are oriented towards a "tutorial" format, requiring the instructor to strictly follow a script. If you deviate from the script or skip a section, the end results do not always match the exercise, which throws the students off. Or the follow-up exercises depended on you completing the previous exercise exactly as specified in order to work.

As a result, the trainer simply becomes a "reader" - meaning you end up reading the exercise almost word-for-word to the student. As long as students can read, they really don't need you unless they deviate from the script and get into trouble.

If you do skip a section or change things around, students get irritated because "that's not the way it is in the book!" Your class is actually being taught by the training manual and not by you!

We believe that **you**, not the manual should be controlling the flow of the class. After all, you are the professional being paid for the training! Every experienced instructor has their own way of teaching a class. You know what exercises are good examples, when to give them and how long to spend on a topic. If a class is slower or faster, you can sense that and can give more exercises as needed or maybe spend a little more time on a topic if the class is a bit slower.

Our courseware is written in the form of a "reference" manual - meaning that the students can use the manual when they return to work/home as a reference rather than a step-by-step tutorial.

Think back for a moment to one of your recent classes where you were teaching from a tutorial manual. Remember that student sitting in the back, not paying attention to a single word you were saying? What was he/she doing? They were reading ahead in the manual, doing every little step in the book as fast as they could read and type! They were so pleased with themselves that they could "read" how to do this program that they missed out on all your great examples, tricks/shortcuts and additional explanations! This happens all of the time with scripted courses. These people don't really learn this way, they just blindly type in commands, not really understanding what they are doing.

This is only one of the many problems that you run into with "tutorial" courseware, but let's focus on the advantages of using our manuals.

ADVANTAGES

There are several advantages to using this format which we have broken down according to three basic categories: students; instructors; and clients.

Advantages for the Student

➢ It's an easy-to-read reference guide. If a student needs to know how to do something, they don't have to read through pages and pages of "Johnny's" letter to mom to figure it out!

Once students leave your class and are dependent upon themselves, they need something that they can use to quickly look up a command or function. Our manual discusses each major topic on a separate page in an easy-to-follow format.

➢ Student notes are in the same book - not written on some pad of paper that they just grabbed for class and will misplace later! How many times have you seen students leave their notes in class after writing down all of the information? But how many manuals are left behind?

The left page of our manual is set aside for the student to be able to write down in their own words what they understand and also any additional information that you might be giving. And it can be written right across from the page of the topic actually being referred to, making it easy to refer back to once class has ended.

➢ Each course can be tailored to the class. Some of the sample exercises in tutorials are so boring or have absolutely nothing in common with the client. Without predefined exercises, you can tailor the course to the client using your examples that you have developed over the years.

Advantages for the Instructor

> Students pay attention. Since they do not really know what you are going to be doing next, students have to follow your instructions. This keeps you in control of the class instead of having students in different parts of the book.

> You can alter the speed of the course as required. As you know, each class progresses differently depending on the various experience levels of the students. If you find you have a faster group, you can give additional exercises or go into more depth for each topic. If you have a slower class, you are not pressured into having to complete all of the "scenarios" or "practice" exercises if you feel you cannot cover them adequately.
>
> Again, you are in control. You can speed up or slow the class down as you see fit. You can expand or condense the amount of information covered on a topic as required.

> You can customize your courses without having to do all the development work! Simply change the exercises to topics that relate more closely to the client. This makes them feel as if you are "customizing" the course for them! We have supplied all of our exercise pages in a separate "Files" folder which may be modified and included with the manuals as the training company sees fit.

Advantages for the Client

> The client is assured of having qualified instructors. Since there are no step-by-step "follow me" type instructions, the instructor must really know the material. How many times have you heard from other instructors how they "winged" it through class by reading the manual? It doesn't take much for someone who does not know the program well to still "teach" a course if they have a step-by-step tutorial to follow!
>
> Would you send that instructor to one of your clients?

> More productive employees. Since students actually have to pay attention, students absorb more of what they do.
>
> Since the class can be customized, the client can be sure that students are learning exactly what they need in order to perform their jobs more efficiently once they return to their workplace.

HOW TO USE THIS MANUAL

This manual was designed to be used as a reference. This is not a step-by-step tutorial. Our feeling is that students did not pay to have someone stand in front of class and <u>read</u> them something that they could do on their own.

Through our own classroom experience, we have discovered that students don't read detailed descriptions and that lengthy text is ignored. They prefer to explore and try things out.

In typical tutorials, students often get lost following rote procedures and get caught in error conditions from which they can't back out of. Besides, once students leave class, they just want something they can use to look up a subject quickly without having to read through an entire tutorial. Our design ensures that each course is stimulating and customized yet covers the outlined objectives.

Keys and commands that you need to press are displayed as icons such as `ENTER` or ⬆.

Each topic starts on a new page, making things easy to find and follow. In addition, topics covering actual commands always begin with the USAGE section where we explain the purpose of the command.

Microsoft Word has more than one method for accessing its commands. You can use the keyboard using a combination of the function keys and shortcuts, or you can use the mouse by accessing the tools on the ribbon.

You can also use your finger (if you are working on a touch screen device). Not knowing which you would prefer, this book has been written emphasizing mouse and touch commands. Keyboard shortcuts are, however, also included.

The next page shows how a typical topic will be discussed and each part found in the book.

THE TOPIC TITLE WILL BE ON TOP

USAGE:

This part of the manual explains what the command is used for, how it works and other miscellaneous information.

This icon indicates tools or buttons to click on with your mouse.

This part lists the keystrokes and function keys the user may press as a shortcut way of performing the command.

Microsoft Word supports a whole host of touch-screen gestures, including the swiping, pinching and rotating motions familiar to smartphone and tablet users. Tapping an item opens it; pressing and holding an item pops up a menu to display more information about it (similar to [RIGHT] clicking). This icon indicates a touch-screen gesture.

NOTE:	*This box will tell of things to watch out for. The symbol in the left column always indicates an important note to remember.*

TIP:	*This box will let you in on a little secret or shortcut. The icon to the left always indicates a "TIP".*

Module One

- **Running Microsoft Word**
- **The Word Screen**
- **Getting Help**
- **Creating a New Document**
- **Changing Views**
- **Saving & Naming a File**
- **Spell Checking**
- **Printing & Previewing Documents**
- **Closing Documents**

RUNNING MICROSOFT WORD

USAGE:

Microsoft Word can be accessed through the Start menu, the Windows desktop or the taskbar (located along the bottom of the desktop window).

 If you have pinned a shortcut to your desktop, click or tap the **Word** icon to run the application.

If you have pinned it to your taskbar, simply click on the Word icon:

If the Word icon isn't located on the desktop, you'll need to display all of your apps (from within the Start menu) to run it.

 Open the Start menu.

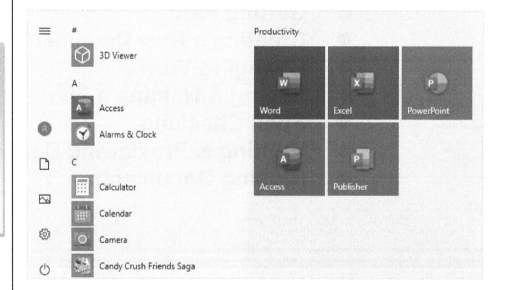

Instructor Note:

After offering a brief overview of the features within Word, have students access the program from the Start Menu.

If it isn't already pinned to the Start menu (along the right), scroll through the alphabetical listing of installed apps or click on a letter to display an alphabetical index where you can quickly get to the app based on the first letter of its name.

THE WORD SCREEN

When you first run Word, the following screen will be displayed:

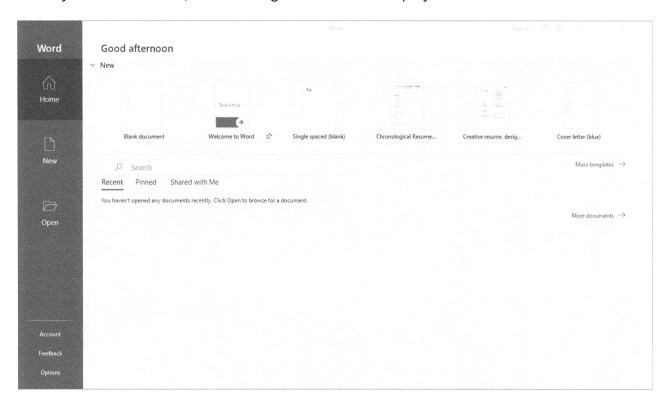

Use **Home** to quickly create a new document or open a recent file.

Use **New** to scroll through all of the templates available within Word. There are several categories of templates (Business, Cards, Flyers, Education, Holidays, Resumes and Cover Letters, Letters).

Use **Open** to browse your system for an existing document.

Once you select an item from the left panel, use the right portion of the window to choose the type of new document you want to open, or create a new document - either a blank one or a new document based on one of the many templates available within Word.

If you choose to create a **blank document**, the following screen will appear:

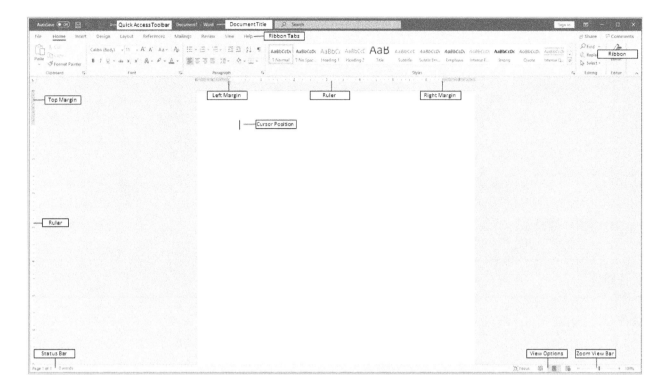

The screen can be quite intimidating the first time you see it as there are so many items displayed on it.

However, if you take a few minutes to familiarize yourself with the various screen elements, the program will become easier to work with.

Along the top left corner of the screen is Save tool as well as the Undo and Redo tools.

Since those are tools that are most often used, they are placed in a convenient location on what is referred to as the "Quick Access Toolbar".

Click or tap on the button to the right of these tools ⏷ to customize this Quick Access Toolbar.

The name of current document followed by the application name is displayed in the middle left portion of the window.

Instructor Note:

The Share option is Microsoft's feature allowing you to more quickly share documents with other users and collaborate in real-time. Be sure to explain this – even though this feature is not covered until the Intermediate class.

The right side of the title bar contains an option to sign in to your Microsoft Office account as well as the Ribbon Display Options button ⬆ and three icons for minimizing, maximizing, and closing:

⬆   —   ⬜   ✕

Share | This icon (on the next line) allows you to work with others simultaneously on a document. Click on it to quickly share the current document. It also offers live document collaboration to view edits made by other users as they happen.

Comments | Allows you to view and respond to comments.

Also on the title bar is a magnifying glass 🔍 to help you to quickly **search** for help topics.

The second line (towards the left) contains tabs used to access a series of **Ribbons** to help you quickly find the commands needed to complete a task. Commands are organized in logical groups collected together under these tabs. Each tab relates to a type of activity. For example, the View tab contains tools to customize the view. To reduce clutter, some tabs are shown only when needed.

Press **CTRL** + **F1** to display/hide the ribbon.

To make it easier to select commands and features, touch screen users can increase the space between buttons. Click or tap on ▼ (on the Quick Access Toolbar) and select Touch/Mouse Mode from the pull-down menu. A new tool will appear on the Quick Access toolbar. Click on 👆 ▾ and choose **Touch** from the pull-down menu to increase the space between buttons on the ribbon.

Use the **ALT** key to access the ribbon directly from the keyboard. For example, if you were to press **ALT** + **N**, you could access the "Insert" ribbon. Each time you press **ALT**, Word displays corresponding letters for the ribbon items to help you to continue using keyboard shortcuts to select them.

Down the right side of the screen is the **scroll bar** used to quickly move (vertically) within your document. Use the arrows located across the top and bottom of the scrollbar to move up and down.

To move more quickly, drag the small rectangle located within the scroll bar to the desired location (up or down). If you zoom to a larger size than can fit horizontally within the window, a horizontal scroll bar will appear across the bottom of the screen.

The **Ruler** indicates the current margins and tab settings and is displayed across the top and along the left side of the typed document. You can toggle the ruler on/off through the View ribbon checkbox ☑ Ruler .

The actual typing area is the large interior portion of the window that the program uses to display its data and special symbols. In Word, this working section is referred to as the **Text Area**.

Within the text area you should see a small blinking vertical line, referred to as the **Insertion Point** or cursor. It marks the spot where your next typed character will appear.

You should also see an **I-beam** I which indicates where the mouse pointer is located. As you move the mouse to the ribbon area at the top of the screen or along the left or right edges of the document, it will change into the shape of an arrow ⇖. The arrow is used to point to items within the ribbon or to select lines of text.

Just below and to the left of the vertical scroll bar is the **Zoom** Area. Notice you can click or tap on the increase **+** or decrease **-** buttons to change the zoom factor. You can also drag the slider horizontally to change the text size as it appears on the screen. Word displays the current percentage just to the left of this area.

To the left of the zoom area are three **View Icons**. These are used to change the current page for display purposes. Simply click or tap on the view you want to switch to. You can remove all menus from the screen by switching to **Focus mode.**

The left side of this line contains the **Status Bar** which indicates the section, number of pages and how many words have been entered in the document, as well as information on proofing tools.

To make working with multiple documents less confusing, Word displays all opened files along the taskbar at the very bottom of the screen. Rather than having to access the ribbon labeled **View** to switch between opened windows, you can use your mouse to click on the name of the file you want to access directly on the taskbar. Once selected, that document becomes the active window.

WORKING WITH HELP

USAGE:

Word offers an extensive help feature without you having to do more than enter the item you need help on.

Using the search bar, you can enter the function or feature you are looking for and Word will offer you the function itself (rather than a help page describing it).

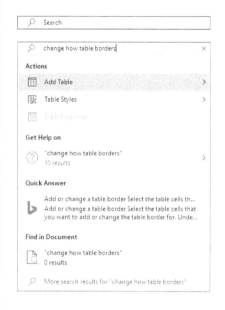

Click or tap in this section (located at the very top of the screen) and type your question.

As soon as you begin typing, Word will display help on that topic.

If Word finds the related commands for that topic, it displays them in the pull-down menu.

If none of the commands listed are what you want, click on the "Get Help on…" item for an additional menu containing more detailed information on the topic you are searching for.

Use the "More results" option (from within the original menu) to search for additional topics that might be related to what you are looking for.

Clicking on one of the items within the "Get Help on …" submenu displays a new panel along the right side of your screen:

This panel displays help on the item you selected.

Scroll through the step-by-step instructions and diagrams.

The article may include links to related help topics. Some links may require Internet access as they will attempt to launch your Internet browser and access Microsoft's support website.

←   Click on this arrow to return to the previous help screen.

⌂   Click on this icon to return to the main help window.

⌕   Click or tap in this box to enter a new search topic.

At the end of each help topic, you will see two items:

One will allow you to send feedback to Microsoft as to whether the information contained within the help panel was helpful:

Was this information helpful?

Yes   No

After answering the question, you can also include a comment as part of the feedback you are sending Microsoft:

Great! Any other feedback?

To protect your privacy, please do not include contact information in your feedback. Review our privacy policy.

Send   No thanks

The second item (at the bottom of the help panel) allows you to launch your Internet browser and view more detailed information on the currently selected topic through Microsoft's support website:

Read article in browser ⟗

You can then use your browser's print option if you'd like to print out information on the selected topic.

Instructor Note:

Since printing has changed in this version, emphasize how you can quickly print a help topic through your Internet browser.

EXITING HELP

 Click or tap this button (located in the top right corner) to **close** the help window and return to your document.

Instructor Note:

Emphasize the importance of using ScreenTips to learn about this – and other MS Office – apps.

SCREENTIPS

A common problem most users encounter is not knowing what each tool on the screen represents.

For example, the SAVE tool is displayed as a 3.5" diskette which some users do not immediately relate to saving a file.

To alleviate this problem, Word offers quick mouse assistance on each tool, referred to as ScreenTips.

As you point to a tool, Word will display a quick note as to the tool's function.

VIEWING OPTIONS

USAGE:

Word provides more than one way to view a document. The five views include Print Layout (the most common), Full Screen Reading, Web Layout, Outline, and Draft. The main difference between these views is your personal preference as to how you want to work with the document. Each view has its own unique format. You can switch between the views at any time. It is also possible to zoom in or out of a document to get different perspectives of the same page.

You can change the display mode by either accessing the "Document Views" section on the **View** ribbon or using the viewing icons located towards the bottom right of the screen, you can switch between the three most popular:

 Click or tap this icon to switch to **Read Mode** view. This view is best when opening a document simply for reading as it hides most of the screen elements.

 Click or tap this button to switch to **Print Layout** view. This display shows the final page layout while still allowing you to edit the document. Headers, footers and all formatting are displayed within this view.

 Click or tap this icon to switch to **Web Layout** view. This display is used to create documents for the Internet.

- + You can use these two buttons (located to the right of the view icons along the bottom right side of the screen) to increase/decrease the zoom factor for the text displayed on the screen. You can also drag the bar in the middle of these two buttons to increase/decrease the zoom factor

100% If you click or tap this button, a dialog box will open for you to select a **Zoom** factor for the text displayed on the screen.

You can also access the "Zoom" section on the **View** ribbon to switch to a specific zoom factor, 100%, one page, two pages, or page width view.

Instructor Note:

Point out that there are only 3 view icons in this version (although there are 5 views).

Previous versions of Word displayed all 5 icons.

Instructor Note:

Even though it's overwhelming to see the nonprinting symbols on the screen (especially at the beginning of this class), show students how to display and then hide them.

DISPLAYING NON-PRINTING SYMBOLS

¶ This tool (located within the Paragraph section on the Home ribbon) toggles between displaying/hiding non-printing symbols, such as hard returns, spaces and tabs.

SHOW/HIDE SCREEN ELEMENTS

The "Show" section on the View ribbon is used to display (when checked) or hide various screen elements. These elements include the ruler (to see your margins), gridlines (to align graphic objects) and the navigation pane (to quickly move through the structural view of your file).

WORKING WITH READ MODE

The full screen "read mode" hides most of the screen elements so that you can easily read only the text within the document. This view is useful when reviewing a document from a colleague.

The only items visible across the top of the screen are the File, Tools and View ribbons along with the name of the document and minimize, restore and close icons along the right.

A new button ⌐┐ is added along the top right side of the screen which allows you to auto-hide the Reading toolbar (to make even more room on your screen for the document).

  While working within the Read Mode, use these buttons to move between pages.

RETURNING THE SCREEN TO NORMAL

 When done reviewing the document in this view, click or tap this button to return to Print Layout view.

CREATING A NEW DOCUMENT

Word places you in a new document as you enter the program. Although the screen may appear to be blank, glancing in the upper portion of the screen (title bar) reminds you that a document is being created.

You may immediately begin typing your file.

PRACTICE EXERCISE

Instructions:	❶	Type in the following paragraphs. Remember not to press the ENTER key except at the end of each paragraph!
	❷	Be sure to leave the errors included within the example as they are since they will be used later to demonstrate the spell checker.

Instructor Note:

Emphasize that this exercise includes misspellings and grammatical errors that they'll need in order to successfully go through the spell-checking feature.

TO ALL EMPLOYES:

As our fiscal year year comes to a close later this month, we ask that each employee keep their overtime hours dowwn to a minimum.

At the moment, our company is on-target to meet it's projected earnngs estimates but we need the assistance of all of our employees to keep costs down. Since overtime is one of our most costly expenditures we incur, we espcially want to ask supervisors in each division to keep overtime hours down.

Thank yu in addvance for your cooperation.

SAVING A DOCUMENT

USAGE:

Instructor Note:

Explain the difference between selecting SAVE and SAVE AS.

After having typed a document, you will want to save it and assign a name that will allow you to easily find it again. If you access the File tab (across the top of the screen in the ribbon section), you will notice two options for saving a document: **Save** and **Save As**.

Save is the normal save feature which will ask you the first time you save a file to assign a name to it. From that point on, choosing SAVE will simply update the file to include the new information. On the other hand, **Save As** saves an existing file under a new name or as a different format to be imported into another program.

 Click or tap the **Save** icon (on the Quick Access Bar).

When you first save a document, you will need to specify where you want to save it:

Instructor Note:

Since this might be new to a lot of users, take your time and go over this first SAVE AS box where you specify where you want to save the document.

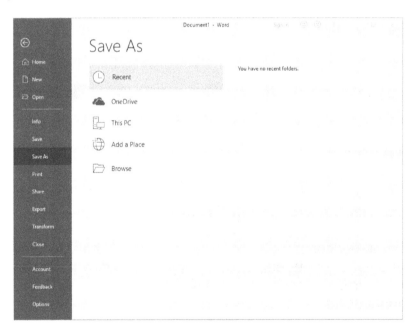

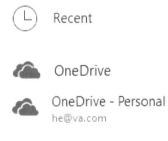 Recent — Use this to save the document in a folder that has been recently used.

OneDrive

OneDrive - Personal
he@va.com — Use this to store the file in your Microsoft OneDrive account instead of your local computer. This allows you to access the file from anywhere. If you are already logged in, you'll see the bottom option.

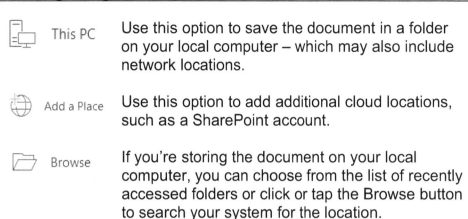

| | This PC | Use this option to save the document in a folder on your local computer – which may also include network locations. |

| | Add a Place | Use this option to add additional cloud locations, such as a SharePoint account. |

| | Browse | If you're storing the document on your local computer, you can choose from the list of recently accessed folders or click or tap the Browse button to search your system for the location. |

Once you select a storage location, you will be taken to the dialog box that will prompt you to enter a file name, as shown below:

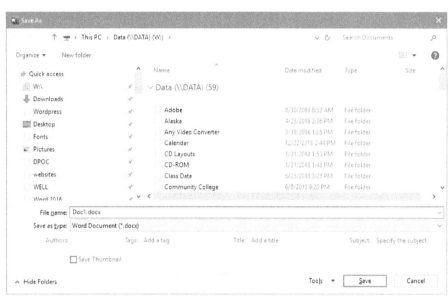

Along the left side of the dialog box, Word displays the **Navigation Pane**. This pane lists common/favorite locations (links) as well as a section for browsing your folders and drives.

You can hide/display the "Folders List" section at the bottom of this area by clicking or tapping on the ∨ ∧ arrows.

Use the address bar to determine the path, as shown below:

Notice the path is displayed horizontally on the bar. For example, in the diagram shown above the currently selected item is the "Data" drive (W:). To get to that folder, you had to first go to "This PC", then the Data drive (W).

This layout is commonly referred to as "bread crumbs" because it shows you the path that was taken to get to the current location.

You can easily move to another folder on the "W" drive by clicking or tapping on the ⟩ arrow beside the drive name and then selecting a different folder to view.

In the box labeled "**File name**", enter a name for the new file. Letters, numbers and spaces are allowed. Enter 1-255 characters.

Notice that Word defaults to assigning the "docx" extension. This is to identify it as a "Microsoft Word" file which has a specific format.

If you want to save the document in another format (such as another word processing application or any previous version of Word so that someone else can edit the document who does not have this version), click or tap on the down arrow ▼ beside the box labeled **Save as type** and select the format from the list provided.

When ready, click or tap [Save] to actually save the document.

> **TIP:** The shortcut key for saving is ⟦CTRL⟧+⟦S⟧.

Instructor Note:

If you had students create the sample in the manual, have them name this document OVERTIME MEMO.

USING THE AUTO SPELL CHECKER

USAGE:

Word offers an automatic spell checker which, as you type, checks words to see if they match the installed dictionary. Simple corrections will be performed automatically for you. If you type a word that is not included in the installed dictionary, Word will flag it as a misspelling by underlining it in red. The underline is for viewing purposes only and will not be printed.

This is a sentence with a mstake in it.

You can quickly correct the spelling mistake using your mouse.

Click the **[RIGHT]** mouse button (or tap and hold if using a touch screen) while pointing to the flagged word. A pop-up menu will appear.

Be sure that **Spelling** (the first option within the pop-up menu) is selected, as shown below:

> **Instructor Note:**
>
> *We'll be covering the grammar checker later in the manual but do mention that blue underlining indicates a grammatical error while red indicates a spelling mistake.*

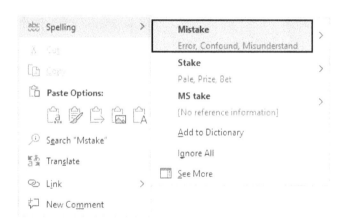

The top portion of the Spelling submenu offers suggestions for the flagged word.

Notice that Word also allows you to **add** the word to the user dictionary for future reference or **ignore** the word (regardless of how many times it is contained within the document).

If you select **See More**, Word will open the Spelling pane within the right section of the window.

USING THE SPELL CHECKER

USAGE:

Before printing and sending a document out for others to read, you should always spell check it for typing errors. By comparing words in your file against the dictionary, Word can check your spelling and alert you of possible mistakes.

For each word the program cannot find in its dictionary, Word asks what to do. You will be able to choose to change the spelling, suggest alternative words, have the word remain as it is, or add the word to the dictionary. Word also checks for words that are incorrectly capitalized and for repeated words.

 If there are spelling and/or grammatical errors flagged within your document, Word will replace the icon (located on the status bar at the bottom of your screen). Click/tap on this icon to open the Editor panel.

 You can also click or tap on the **Editor** tool to review your entire document.

Editor

Word will open the Editor panel and display an overview of the spelling and grammatical issues it finds within your document:

The top section of the Editor panel includes a button showing the total number of results (possible errors) within your document. Click/tap on this button to cycle through all the possible errors Word has flagged.

In the **Corrections** section, you will see the number of spelling and/or grammatical errors that have been flagged.

The **Refinements** section displays the number of suggested changes to make your document clearer and more concise.

Click on **Spelling** to cycle through the spelling errors.

Word displays the flagged word and its surrounding text:

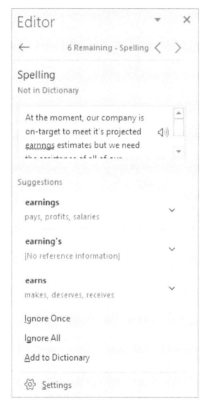

Click on to hear the error out loud.

Below the error, Word lists suggested corrections (along with synonyms).

If one of the suggestions is correct, click or tap on the correct spelling. If you are afraid you misspelled a word more than once, click on the down arrow beside the correct spelling and choose **Change All**.

Within that same pull-down, you can also have the correct word read out loud or spelled out loud.

If this is a word you misspell often, you can have Word **AutoCorrect** it in the future as you type.

If you want to keep the existing spelling, select **Ignore Once**. If the word in question appears throughout the document, you can choose to **Ignore All**.

To add the word to your custom dictionary for future reference, (i.e., your company name), choose **Add to Dictionary**.

✖ Click or tap this button to remove the panel from the screen. After running the spell checker, save your document again.

PRINTING YOUR DOCUMENT

USAGE:

Obviously, you'll need to print at some point. You can choose what part of the document to print (such as the current page, multiple pages or the entire file). In addition, you can specify which printer to use and how many copies you'd like.

Click or tap the **File** tab on the ribbon and select **Print** from the pull-down list of options.

Instructor Note:

Whether the students are connected to a printer or not, be sure to take them into this dialog box and discuss each of the print options.

The Print window will be displayed:

Instructor Note:

Take your time and go over each and every option within this box.

Printing is important and you want the students to leave feeling very confident that they can print and are familiar with the various print options.

A preview of the document as it will be printed appears along the right side of this window.

 52% — | — +   Use this section to zoom in and out of the document.

     Use this button to quickly display the full page.

◀ 5 of 15 ▶   Use this section to move between pages within the print preview.

 Brother MFC-9325CW Printer / Ready   Click or tap this button to select the printer you want to use.

Printer Properties   Click or tap this item to access additional settings for the printer.

 Print All Pages / The whole thing   Use this section to specify which page(s) should be printed.

 Print One Sided / Only print on one side of th...   Specify whether you want a single-sided or double-sided printout.

 Collated / 1,2,3 1,2,3 1,2,3   You can choose to collate multi-page documents so that you don't have to go back and arrange them manually.

 Portrait Orientation   Choose whether you are printing landscape or portrait.

 Letter / 8.5" x 11"   Use this section to specify your paper size.

 Normal Margins / Left: 1" Right: 1"   Set your margins for the printout.

 1 Page Per Sheet   If you're creating a booklet, you may need this to combine pages on a single sheet.

Page Setup   Provides detailed document settings.

 Print   Click or tap this button to begin printing.

TIP: To quickly print directly from within the document, press **CTRL** + **P**.

CLOSING A DOCUMENT

USAGE:

Although you can have several windows (documents) open at the same time, it is usually a good idea to close a file once you have saved and printed it if you no longer need to continue editing.

✕ Click or tap the close button in the upper right corner of the window to close the current document. If you only have one document open and you click or tap this icon, Word will close the entire program.

If you only have one document open and don't want to close the entire application, you can close the document by accessing the **File** tab on the ribbon, as shown below:

Select **Close** from the pull-down list of options.

NOTE:	*If you have made changes to the file and have not saved those changes, Word will ask whether you want to save the changes before closing the file.*

CREATING A NEW DOCUMENT

USAGE:

If you are in the midst of working with one file and then decide to create another document, you will need to instruct Word as to what type of new document you want to create.

To create a new document, select **New** from the pull-down list of options within the File tab on the ribbon.

> **Instructor Note:**
>
> *Templates are discussed in the "If You Have Time" module and within the Intermediate class so don't go into detail here.*
>
> *Do explain that every new document is based on a template and that the default one is labeled "**Blank document**".*

The following window will be displayed:

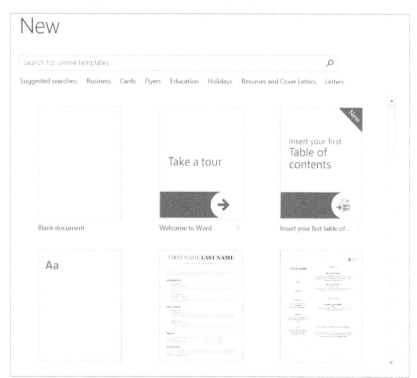

You can create a blank document or base the new file on one of the built-in templates that come with Word. A template is used to determine the basic structure of the document and can contain predefined settings, such as colors, fonts, page layouts, graphics, formatting and macros.

If there are templates that you'll be using on a regular basis, you may want to pin them to the list so that they remain at the top for easy access.

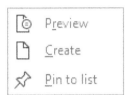

To quickly pin a template, point to the template and then click or tap on (located along the bottom right corner of its preview or click your [RIGHT] mouse button once and choose **Pin to list** from the pop-up menu.

If you change your mind, click or tap on the icon (located on the template) to unpin the template.

To actually use one of the templates, click on the one you want to use. A pop-up window is displayed with a preview of the template, a short description, and its size.

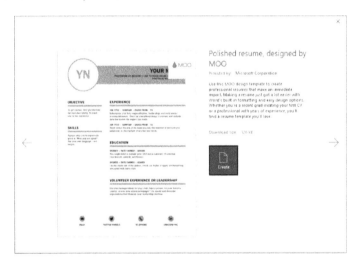

Click or tap this button to create a new document based on the selected template.

> **NOTE:** To create a new blank document without accessing the menu, press **CTRL**+**N** from within a document.

Instructor Note:

Point out how to quickly pop between multiple documents and let students try it out.

Have them create two or three new documents based on various templates and then pop between them.

SWITCHING BETWEEN MULTIPLE DOCUMENTS

When working with two or more open documents, you can switch between them by accessing the **View** ribbon and then clicking on the button labeled **Switch Windows.**

Alternatively, you can quickly switch between open documents using the Windows taskbar (located along the bottom of your screen):

Either point or click on the Word icon to display a small preview of each of your opened documents, as shown below:

As you hover your mouse over a document preview, Windows will display that window.

Next, simply click the document you wish to work with.

PRACTICE EXERCISE

Instructions:		
	❶	Create the following document.
	❷	Spell check the file to locate any mistakes you may have made.
	❸	Save the file as **AUDIT**
	❹	Print (or preview) the file.
	❺	Close the file.

Mr. James Doe
Anderson Accounting Firm
111 West 57th Street, Suite 1500
New York, NY 10014

Dear Mr. Doe,

I am writing on behalf of my company to thank you for the work your accounting firm did for us last month during our audit.

Because of your experience in the matter along with detailed record-keeping on our part, we passed with flying colors.

What could have been a stressful situation turned out to be quite simple. Your firm is largely responsible for that outcome.

Thank you again for your assistance. I hope that our companies can continue to do business in the future.

Sincerely,

Sally Smith
Vice President of Operations

Module Two

- **Opening an Existing Document**
- **Movement Keys**
- **Insert vs. Typeover**
- **Deleting Text**
- **Undeleting Text**

OPENING AN EXISTING DOCUMENT

USAGE:

When you want to work on a document that already exists, you will need to open it. If it's a file that you have been working on, you can select it from a list of recent files.

To open an existing document, select **Open** from the pull-down list of options within the File tab on the ribbon.

Instructor Note:

Since you should have already discussed how to move between drives and folders in the Save dialog box, have students tell YOU how to do it.

The following window will be displayed:

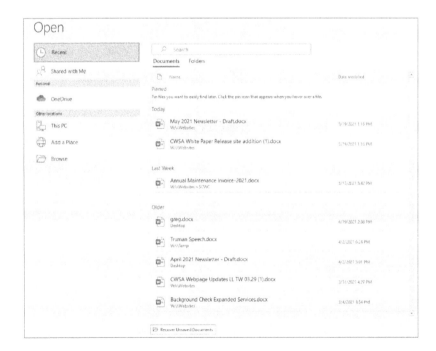

Notice your most recently accessed files are listed in this window.

Your first step is to select where the file is stored:

🕐	Recent	This is the default option. Word automatically displays files you have recently been working on so that you can quickly return to them.
👤	Shared with Me	If you are signed in to your Microsoft account, you can use this option to access documents that have been shared with you.
☁	OneDrive	Use this if you want to open a document that has been stored on the Internet rather than a local computer.
🖥	This PC	Use this option to open a document that was stored in a folder on your local computer – which may also include network locations.
🌐	Add a Place	Use this to add a new OneDrive or SharePoint location from which to open documents.

> **TIP:** If there are documents or folders that you access often, you can "**pin**" them to the list so that they are always available, whenever you access the Open dialog box.
>
> To pin a document/folder, point to it (from within the list) and then click or tap on the icon.
>
> If you change your mind and no longer need the document/folder pinned to the list, point to the item and then click or tap on ⊤ to remove it.

📂	Browse	If you're opening a document that was stored on your local computer, you can choose from the list of recently accessed folders or click or tap the Browse button to search your system for the folder storing the document.

Once you specify where the document is located, the following dialog box will be displayed:

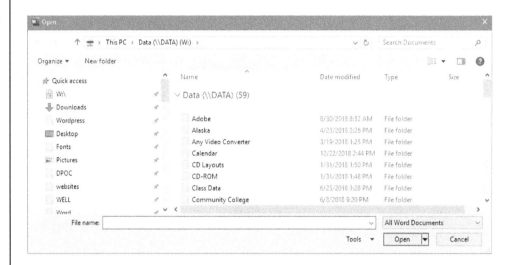

Along the left side of the dialog box, Word displays the **Navigation Pane**. This pane lists common/favorite locations (links) as well as a section for browsing your folders and drives. You can hide/display the "Folders List" section at the bottom of this area by clicking or tapping on the ∨ ∧ arrows.

The address bar is displayed, as shown below:

Notice that the path is displayed horizontally on the bar. For example, in the diagram shown above the currently selected item is the "Data" drive (W) which is part of your computer. To get to that folder, you had to first choose your computer, then the Data drive (W). You could then select the folder containing your Word documents.

This layout is commonly referred to as "bread crumbs" because it shows you the path that was taken to get to the current location and how to get back to the main folder.

In the example shown on the previous page, you can easily move to another folder on the "W" drive by clicking or tapping on ⟩ beside the drive name and then selecting a different folder to view.

Across the top of the window are the following buttons:

Organize ▼   Click or tap this button to access the **Organize** pull-down menu. From the pull-down list, select the operation (e.g., cut, copy, paste, delete, rename) you want to perform on existing files listed within this box.

New folder   Click or tap this button to create a new folder.

When ready, double-click or double-tap on the name of the file you want to open or highlight the name and click or tap | Open ▼|

| Open |
| Open Read-Only |
| Open as Copy |
| Open in Browser |
| Open with Transform |
| Open in Protected View |
| Open and Repair |

If you click or tap the down arrow ▼ beside | Open ▼|, you can choose from a list of options (such as opening the file as read-only or in your Web browser).

| **TIP:** | *To open more than one file at a time, select the first file by clicking on its name once to highlight it. Next, hold the CTRL key down as you click or tap each additional file to be opened. Once all files have been selected, click or tap | Open ▼| to actually open them. Each file will be placed in its own window.* |

| **TIP:** | *The shortcut key for opening files is CTRL + O.* |

Welcome back!
Pick up where you left off:

THE WORD SCREEN
Saturday

When you open an existing document, Word asks if you want to pick up where you left off. If you are working on a large multi-page document, that feature can be extremely helpful. If the message disappears, look for the tab ⌐ and click on it to be taken to your last editing section.

NAVIGATING WITHIN A DOCUMENT

USAGE:

When working with large files you should know the quickest ways of moving from page to page and from one area to another.

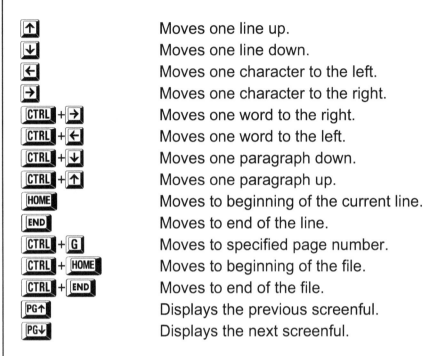

↑	Moves one line up.
↓	Moves one line down.
←	Moves one character to the left.
→	Moves one character to the right.
CTRL + →	Moves one word to the right.
CTRL + ←	Moves one word to the left.
CTRL + ↓	Moves one paragraph down.
CTRL + ↑	Moves one paragraph up.
HOME	Moves to beginning of the current line.
END	Moves to end of the line.
CTRL + G	Moves to specified page number.
CTRL + HOME	Moves to beginning of the file.
CTRL + END	Moves to end of the file.
PG↑	Displays the previous screenful.
PG↓	Displays the next screenful.

Instructor Note:

Spend some time now reviewing the keyboard shortcuts.

Most students never learn the keyboard shortcuts but when typing, it makes sense to use them.

To scroll through the document using the mouse, click or tap one of the arrows located on either the horizontal or vertical scroll bar.

If you drag the scroll box on the vertical scroll bar up or down, Word will display the current page number to the left of the box. When you see the desired page, release the mouse button and that page will be displayed.

If you are using a mouse with a scroll wheel, roll the rubber wheel (located between the **[LEFT]** and **[RIGHT]** mouse buttons) forward or back to quickly scroll through large documents.

NOTE:	*If you are using the mouse to move through a document, remember that you must click on the new page before the cursor will move to the new location!*

If you click or tap on the left side of the status line where the current page number and section are displayed (located at the bottom of your screen), Word will ask what page to "Go To".

　　　　　　　　　　　　　　　　　　　　　　©2021 EZ-REF Courseware

REPLACING TEXT

USAGE:

In Word you are automatically placed in insert mode. If you move your cursor to a line where text exists and begin typing, Word will insert it and move the existing text over.

REPLACING EXISTING TEXT

There will be times when you would rather type over existing text.

To do this, select the text to be replaced as described below:

Move to the beginning of the text to be selected and then drag to highlight the desired text.

Move the cursor to the beginning of the text to be selected. Hold the SHIFT key down and use the arrow keys to highlight text.

After you have selected the text, begin typing. The highlighted text will be replaced by the new information.

> *Instructor Note:*
>
> *Have students type a sentence. Then add a word between existing words and then replace a word.*
>
> *For example…*
>
> *Word will improve your productivity.*
>
> *Word will drastically improve your productivity.*
>
> *Word will increase your productivity.*

DELETING TEXT

USAGE:

Instructor Note:

This is another page containing shortcuts that most users don't know.

Take your time and show students to pay attention to what their mouse pointer looks like before clicking.

When a block of text is no longer needed, you can easily remove it.

 Deletes the character to the left of the cursor. Works like a correctable backspace on a typewriter.

[DEL] Deletes the character to the right of the cursor.

SELECTING WITH THE MOUSE

Word Double-Click or Double-Tap on the word.

Line Move the mouse pointer to the left of a line until it changes to an arrow. Click or tap once.

Sentence Hold the **[CTRL]** key down and click the mouse button anywhere on the sentence.

Paragraph Move the mouse pointer to the left of a line until it changes to a pointer arrow. Double-Click or Double-Tap. Triple-Clicking or Triple-Tapping on a paragraph also selects it.

Any Text Move the mouse pointer to the beginning of the block you want to delete. Click or tap and drag.

Entire File Move the mouse pointer to the left of a line until it changes to a pointer arrow. Hold **[CTRL]** down and click once. Triple-Clicking or Triple-Tapping on the left side of the screen also selects the entire file. You can also press **[CTRL]** + **[A]** to select the entire document.

 You can also use this button (located within the **Editing** section of the Home ribbon) to select items. The pull-down list includes options for selecting everything within the document, graphic objects, or text with similar formatting.

After selecting the item(s) you wish to remove, press **[DEL]**.

SELECTING NONCONTIGUOUS TEXT

To select multiple pieces of text from different parts of a document, you will need to select the first item and then, while holding down the **CTRL** key, select the additional text items. For example, to select three words that are located in different paragraphs, double-click or double-tap on the first word and then while holding down the **CTRL** key, double-click or double-tap on the other two words. All three words will be highlighted.

USING THE KEYBOARD TO SELECT TEXT

Hold down **SHIFT** and use the arrows to highlight desired text.

To highlight larger blocks of text, you can use the movement keys while holding **SHIFT**.

Below is a listing of some quick selecting keys:

SHIFT + **CTRL** + **→**	Selects to the next word.
SHIFT + **CTRL** + **←**	Selects to the previous word.
SHIFT + **END**	Selects to the end of a line.
SHIFT + **HOME**	Selects to the beginning of a line.
SHIFT + **CTRL** + **↓**	Selects to the end of the paragraph.
SHIFT + **CTRL** + **↑**	Selects to the beginning of the paragraph.
SHIFT + **CTRL** + **END**	Selects to the end of the document.
SHIFT + **CTRL** + **HOME**	Selects to the beginning of the document.

Instructor Note:

Most students will prefer using the mouse to select text but show them these shortcuts quickly – just so they know that they exist.

Once the appropriate block of text is selected, press **DEL** to remove the selected block of text.

OOPS!! UNDELETING TEXT

USAGE:

If you ever delete a portion of a document by mistake, Word has the ability to undo the deletion. Undo instructs the program to disregard the last action (whether it was deleting, copying, or applying format changes). It is important to understand, however, that certain actions (such as printing and saving) cannot be undone. Word has the capability of remembering not only the last action performed but the last several.

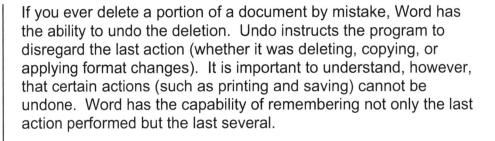 Click or tap the **Undo** tool to undo the last action.

| Clear |
| Spelling Change |
| Typing 'with a mstake in it.' |
| AutoCorrect |
| Typing 'This is a sentnce ' |
| Cancel |

If you click or tap on the down arrow ▾ (to the right of the tool), you can scroll through the last several actions.

Move down the list to highlight the number of actions to undo. They must be done in sequence!

REDOING/REPEATING COMMANDS

If you undo an action and then change your mind (again), you can always redo what you have just undone.

Click or tap this button to redo the last undo.

The Redo button (shown above) changes from **Redo** to **Repeat** depending on what action was last performed. For example, if you just deleted an item and then chose to "Undo" the deletion, Word would display the "Redo" button. However, if you just applied an attribute (such as bold or underline) to a block of text, Word would display the "Repeat" button so that you could repeat the last action (applying the attribute) for another block of text.

USING CLICK AND TYPE

USAGE:

Word has a feature referred to as **Click and Type** which allows you to simply double-click at a blank location and begin typing. Depending on where you click (left, center or right), Word will automatically apply the formatting necessary to align the new item to the position where you double-clicked.

If you double-click in a blank spot when your mouse pointer looks like this, the next item you enter will be left-justified.

If you double-click in a blank spot when your mouse pointer looks like this, Word will automatically indent the first line of new text you enter and left-justify the remainder of the paragraph. This pointer will only appear when your mouse pointer is approximately a half-inch from the left margin.

If you double-click in a blank spot when your mouse pointer looks like this, the next item you enter will be centered.

If you double-click in a blank spot when your mouse pointer looks like this, the next item you enter will be right-justified.

Instructor Note:

These can be a bit tricky so take your time and make sure students actually see each of these.

In the example below, turning on the formatting marks shows how 'Click and Type' adds the blank lines and justification codes:

PRACTICE EXERCISE

Instructions:	❶	Open the file **AUDIT**. Make the necessary revisions so that the document is the same as the one shown below.
	❷	When you are done, save and print (or preview) the file.

Mr. John Doe
Sanderson Accounting Firm
111 West 57th Street, Suite 1500
New York, NY 10014

Dear Mr. Doe,

I am writing on behalf of my company to let you know that we will no longer be doing business with your firm.

Because of your inexperience in the matter along with messy record-keeping on our part, we failed to provide the necessary paperwork needed to pass the audit.

What could have been a simple matter has now turned into an accounting nightmare. Your firm is largely responsible for that outcome.

Although I realize there was no malice intended on your part, I want you to know that we will not be continuing our working relationship with your firm.

Sincerely,

Sally Smith
Vice President of Operations

Module Three

- **Applying Attributes**
- **Changing Fonts & Point Size**
- **The Format Painter & Highlighter Pen**
- **Changing the Page Setup**
- **Adjusting Margins**
- **Adjusting Line Spacing**
- **Setting Justification**
- **Changing Case**
- **Inserting the Date & Time**

APPLYING ATTRIBUTES

USAGE:

As you enter and edit text, you can change its appearance to add emphasis. Formatting the text means setting the font and size of the letters, and emphasizing words using such attributes as bold, underline or italics. To format characters you can either use the keyboard or the **Home** ribbon. All of the character attributes are located within the "Font" section on this ribbon.

Before typing, turn on the attribute and then begin entering text. When you want to turn the attribute off, select the same tool.

B   Click or tap this tool to turn **bold** on and off.

I   Click or tap this tool to turn *italics* on and off.

U ▾   Click or tap this tool to turn underline on and off. Click on the down arrow ▾ beside the tool to change the underline style.

ab   Click or tap this tool to turn ~~strikeout~~ on and off.

x_2 Click or tap this tool to turn subscript on and off.

x^2 Click or tap this tool to superscript on and off.

A ▾   Use this tool to select from a variety of text effects.

✎ ▾   Click or tap this tool to add a highlight color to a block of text.

A ▾   Click or tap this tool to change the font color.

A^ A˅ Use these tools to **increase**/decrease the font size.

Aa ▾   Click or tap this tool to specify UPPER/lower case.

When you select a block of text, a "mini" toolbar is displayed which provides quick access to fonts, font styles, font sizing, alignment, text color, indent levels, and bullet features.

When you see the mini toolbar, simply point to the attribute you want to set and select it with your mouse.

TURNING HIGHLIGHT ON/OFF

When working on a document, you may want to highlight text so that it stands out - just as you would with a yellow highlighter pen.

To highlight existing text, follow these four steps:

Instructor Note:

Point out that this can be a great tool when editing a document you are working on with another user.

❶ Click or tap the down arrow ⊡ beside the **Text Highlight** tool on the **Home** ribbon.

❷  Select the color you want to use (from the pull-down list) to highlight text.

❸ When you move to your document, the mouse pointer will have changed shape. Click or tap and then drag to select the text to be highlighted.

❹ Click or tap the **Highlight** tool a second time to turn it off.

NOTE:	*If you do not have any text selected before clicking on the Highlighter Pen, the mouse pointer will automatically change to the pen so that you may begin highlighting blocks of text. When done, select the Highlighter Pen tool a second time to turn it off.*

Below is a table summarizing the basic character formatting key combinations:

WHILE HOLDING CTRL	
TAP THIS KEY	**RESULT**
B	Bold
I	Italics
U	Underline
WHILE HOLDING CTRL + SHIFT	
TAP THIS KEY	**RESULT**
D	Double Underline
H	Hidden
K	Small Caps
W	Word Underline

REMOVING ATTRIBUTES

After selecting the text containing the attributes (bold, italics, etc.) you want removed, click on the **Clear Formatting** tool (located within the Font section on the Home ribbon).

You can also press CTRL + SPACEBAR to remove most attributes.

CHANGING FONTS & POINT SIZE

USAGE:

A font is a family of characters that have the same design. To change fonts, you select the new font by its name.

❶ Click or tap the down arrow ⊡ to the right of the **Font** tool (located within the Font section on the Home ribbon).

> Arial ▾

❷ Select the new font from the pull-down list. Notice how Word displays a sample of each font within the pull-down list so that you can see the font before actually selecting it.

❸ The new font begins at the current cursor location and continues until the end of the document or until you change it again. Begin typing your text.

NOTE:	Notice that Word displays the current theme fonts along with the last few selected fonts at the top of the list for easy access.

NOTE:	To change existing text, be sure to select the text first and then choose the desired font. If text is selected, as you scroll through the list of available fonts, Word will display the selected text with the currently highlighted font – as a preview.

CHANGING THE POINT SIZE

❶ Click or tap the down arrow ⊡ to the right of the **Font Size** button (located within the Font section on the Home ribbon).

❷ Select the desired font size from the pull-down list.

❸ The new font size begins at the current cursor location and continues until the end of the document or until you change it again. Begin typing your text.

NOTE:	*As was the case with attributes, to change existing text, be sure to select the text first and then choose the desired font size.*

You can also use the following tools (both of which are located within the Font section on the Home ribbon) to quickly increase or decrease the font size.

 Click or tap these tools to quickly increase or decrease the current font size.

CHANGING THE COLOR OF THE FONT

Although Word defaults to printing your text in black, if you have a color printer, you can change the color of the text by accessing the Home ribbon, as shown in the steps below:

❶ 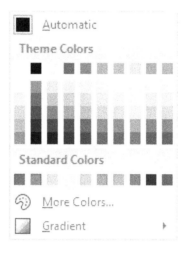 Click or tap this tool to use the last selected color or click on the down arrow ⏷ beside the **Font Color** tool (located within the Font section on the Home ribbon) to choose another font color.

❷ Select the color you want to use (from the pull-down list) for the selected text.

❸ The new text color begins at the current cursor location and continues until the end of the document or until you change it again. Begin typing your text.

> **NOTE:** *To change existing text, be sure to select the text first and then choose the desired color. If text is selected, as you scroll through the list of colors, Word will display the selected text with the currently highlighted color – as a preview.*

> **NOTE:** *The color you chose last becomes the default. If you look at the tool, the current color will be shown (as an underline for the letter A on the tool).*

To view the complete color palette, click or tap on 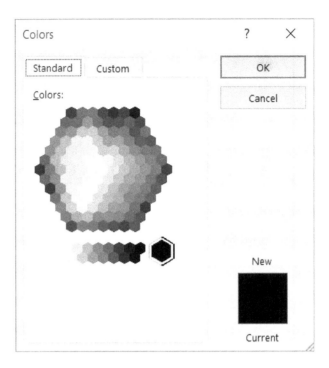 More Colors...

The following dialog box will be displayed:

The first tab (labeled **Standard**) allows you to select from a group of predefined colors.

The box in the lower right corner of the dialog box will display the current font color as well as the new color you select.

The second color tab (labeled **Custom**) allows you to further customize the color applied to the text, as shown below:

Unless you know the exact values for a particular color, follow the steps shown below to choose a custom color:

❶ Click or tap in the palette area on the color to customize. Notice the bottom right corner of the screen contains a box labeled **Current**. Be sure you see the color to customize in that box before continuing to the second step.

❷ Drag the luminance marker ◄ (along the right side of the colors) up or down to brighten or darken the color. Notice the **New** color box at the bottom of the dialog box.

❸ Once you have the desired color, click or tap on the OK button to close the dialog box.

APPLYING TEXT EFFECTS

You can also add special effects to text (such as a shadow or an outline) by accessing the Text Effects tool located on the Home ribbon, as shown in the steps below:

❶ 〔A▾〕 Click or tap on this tool to choose from a list of built-in text effects.

❷ From the list provided, select the effect you want to use.

❸ The new text effect begins at the current cursor location and continues until the end of the document or until you change it again. Begin typing your text.

NOTE:	To change existing text, be sure to select the text first and then choose the desired effect. If text is selected, as you scroll through the list of effects, Word will display the selected text with the currently highlighted effect – as a preview.

ADVANCED FORMATTING OPTIONS

USAGE:

To access the more advanced text effects, you will need to access the "Font" dialog box.

Click or tap the **Font Dialog Box Launcher** (located on the Home ribbon).

The first tab (labeled **Font**) offers the following options:

As you make changes within this dialog box, a preview of your selections is displayed at the bottom.

Font	Scroll through the list of available fonts. They are listed in alphabetical order and contain the fonts currently installed on your system. Click or tap on the font you would like to use.
Font style	Scroll through the list of font styles. The styles available will depend on the currently selected font. Click or tap the style you want to apply.
Size	Scroll through the list of available font sizes. Click or tap on the size you want to apply.
Font color	Click or tap this box to specify which font color to apply to your text.
Underline style	Click or tap this box to specify the type of underline you want to apply to your text.
Underline color	If you have chosen to underline text, you can click on this box to specify which underline color you would like to apply to your text.
Effects	Use these checkboxes to specify which (if any) effects should be applied to your text. To preview each effect, click or tap in its corresponding box (to enable it) and then look at the Preview section (located at the bottom of the dialog box). To remove an unwanted effect, click or tap a second time to remove the check which will disable the effect.
Preview	This section simply displays a preview of the currently selected options within this dialog box to let you see how the text will appear if you accept the current settings.
Set As Default	Click or tap this button to change the default font for all future documents or just your current document.
Text Effects...	Click or tap this button to access a second box containing more advanced text effects.

The tab labeled **Advanced** contains these options:

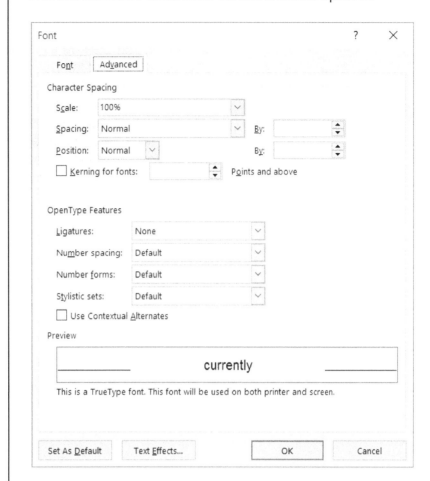

The following options are available within this box:

Scale   Click or tap on the down arrow ⌄ beside this box to stretch or compress the text as a percentage of what it currently is set to.

Spacing   Use this section to manually increase or decrease the spacing between the individual characters.

                      Choose either Expanded or Condensed and then enter the amount in the box labeled **By**.

Position   Use this section to raise or lower the selected text in relation to the baseline.

Choose either Raised or Lowered and then enter the amount in the box labeled **By**.

Kerning for fonts   Use this box to have Word automatically adjust the spacing between characters to give your words a more evenly spaced appearance.

Preview   This section displays a preview of the currently selected options within this dialog box.

OpenType Features   If you are using OpenType fonts, you can use this section to customize the settings for these fonts.

When done, click or tap [OK] to accept the changes made within the dialog box and return to your document.

USING THE FORMAT PAINTER

USAGE:

Word offers a feature which allows you to copy attributes from one block of text and paste them onto another block. This feature can save you time by copying the format of an existing block of text.

To use the format painter, follow the steps outlined below:

❶ Select the text containing the attributes to be copied.

❷ ✂ Format Painter Select the **Format Painter** tool from the Home ribbon. If you plan on formatting more than one block of text, double-click or double-tap on this tool.

Your mouse pointer changes to a paintbrush.

❸ Highlight the block of text to be formatted. Word will automatically apply the same formatting options you copied. If you only clicked the tool once, Word deactivates this feature after the first block is formatted.

❹ If you double-clicked or double-tapped the icon to begin with, the Format Painter remains active until you deactivate it by clicking the tool again.

Continue highlighting each block of text to be formatted.

Instructor Note:

A good example of why you might need this feature is if you're creating a large document containing multiple headings.

Each heading should be uniform in its look.

TIP:	*If you include the end of paragraph marker when you are selecting the block to be copied, Word will also copy any paragraph formats (e.g., spacing, justification) along with any character formats.*

PAGE SETUP

USAGE:

To change the margins, page orientation, and page size or other features that affect the layout of your page, switch to the **Layout** ribbon.

CHANGING MARGINS

Margins
▼

Click or tap the **Margins** tool (located within the Page Setup section on the Layout ribbon).

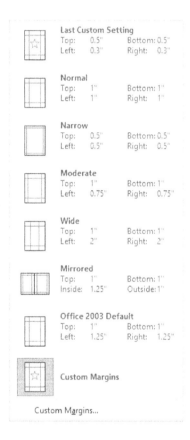

Select the new margin setting from the list provided.

If you need a margin setting that is not included in this pull-down list, click or tap on **Custom Margins…** (located at the bottom of the list) to open a dialog box where you can enter custom margins.

CHANGING ORIENTATION

Click or tap the **Orientation** tool (located within the Page Setup section on the Layout ribbon).

Select the page orientation from the two diagrams provided.

CHANGING PAPER SIZE

Click or tap the **Size** tool (located within the Page Setup section on the Layout ribbon).

Select the paper size desired. If you don't see a size in the list, click on **More Paper Sizes...** to access the Page Setup dialog box.

ACCESSING THE PAGE SETUP DIALOG BOX

To access all the page setup features, click or tap the **Page Setup Dialog Box Launcher** (located on the Layout ribbon).

Instructor Note:

Show students how to make all of their changes right here in this dialog box.

A preview section is provided which is helpful but the ruler is easier to use because you see your document immediately adjusted right in front of you as you are making the changes.

Using the first tab within this dialog box (labeled **Margins**), you can adjust the top, bottom, left or right margins. A preview box is provided in the lower portion of this box to see how your new margin settings will affect the document.

The **Gutter** option refers to an additional margin used when creating manuals or documents which will be bound. This margin is <u>added</u> to either the left or top margins to compensate for binding that may occur. Use this section to specify both the gutter margin and the gutter position.

The **Orientation** option can be changed simply by clicking on the appropriate diagram.

The section labeled **Pages** is used to specify how your multi-page document will be handled. Mirror margins are used when creating books/manuals. While reading a book, margins mirror themselves as the pages are turned to accommodate the binding of the book. For example, even pages might have a left margin of 2" and a right margin of 1" while odd pages would have exactly the opposite settings. When you select this option, left and right margins are replaced by inside and outside margin settings.

You can select the option of 2 pages per sheet if you want to combine two pages of text on a single sheet of paper. Word will do this by adjusting your margins so that two pages can fit on one. Once Word adjusts the margins, you will probably need to review the document to make sure the pages have been split properly.

If you are creating a booklet with more than two pages, choose the book fold option to print your document in landscape format with two pages per sheet. After selecting this option, you can choose to limit each booklet to a specific number of pages. If your document contains more pages than you specify per booklet, Word will print multiple booklets.

The **Apply to** section of the dialog box allows you to apply the margin settings to various portions of the document.

To change the paper size and/or paper source, select the second tab at the top of the dialog box, labeled **Paper**.

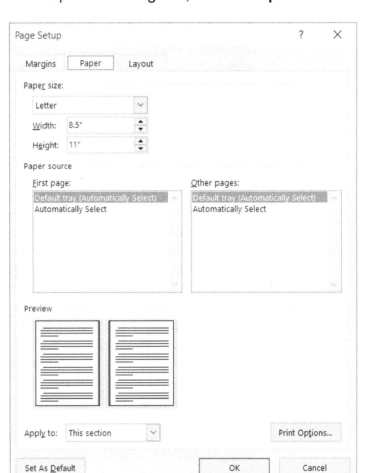

Click or tap the down arrow ⌄ to the right of the **Paper size** box to select from one of many predefined sizes.

You can define a custom size by entering a new width or height in the sections provided.

Using the **Paper source** section, you can instruct Word as to where paper should be loaded from.

For example, your printer may have two paper trays. The first page of a document may require letterhead paper (which is stored in the top paper tray) while the remainder of the document requires bond paper (stored in the bottom tray). Select the tray to be used for the first page as well as the tray to be used for all other pages.

The **Apply to** section of the dialog box allows you to apply the margin settings to various portions of the document.

Click or tap Print Options... to access a second dialog box where you can even further specify how the document will be printed.

You can also control advanced layout settings for headers and footers, section breaks, vertical alignment and line numbers. Be sure the **Layout** tab has been selected from the top of this box.

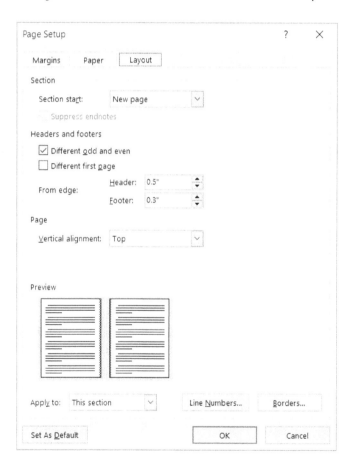

Use **Section start** to select whether the current section should begin on a new, even or odd page, a new column or whether the section should continue from the previous one.

Check the box labeled **Suppress endnotes** if you want to prevent endnotes from printing in the current section. Instead, they will be printed in the next section. Endnotes (like footnotes) are used to explain, comment on, or provide references for text within a document. Whereas footnotes are printed at the bottom of each page, endnotes are typically printed at the end of a document or the end of a section.

Use the section labeled **Header and footers** to determine if you would like different ones added for odd/even pages and whether to have a separate header/footer for the first page.

The section labeled **From edge** is used to define header and footer margins. These two margins are measured from the edge of the paper - within the page margins you have set.

Use **Vertical alignment** to determine whether the text on the page is to be vertically centered or evenly justified between the top and bottom margins.

The **Apply to** section of the dialog box allows you to apply the margin settings to various portions of the document.

Click or tap Line Numbers... to access a second box where you can add or remove line numbering as well as specify what number to start with, the increment to be used, and whether numbering should re-start for each page, each section, or continue until to the end of the document.

Click or tap on Borders... to access a second box which provides options for adding borders and shading to your text and/or pages.

If the changes you make are to be permanent for the current and all future documents (based on this template), click or tap Set As Default

You will need to confirm this option.

Once settings have been changed, select OK to close the "Page Setup" dialog box and return to your document.

CHANGING MARGINS WITH THE MOUSE

USAGE:

Instructor Note:

Emphasize how important it is to pay attention to what it is you're grabbing before you start dragging.

Students often grab the first line indent by mistake – instead of the left margin.

You can easily set all four margins using the mouse. However, be sure you are in Print Layout view before continuing.

❶ Move your mouse to either the horizontal ruler (to adjust left/right margins) or the vertical ruler (to adjust top/bottom margins). The pointer will change to one of these two shapes (depending on which margin is being changed). If you leave your pointer in place for a few seconds, a small note will appear - indicating which margin you have selected (e.g., top or left).

When selecting the left margin marker, you may find the indent markers to be in the way. Place your mouse pointer between the first line indent and hanging indent markers (point more towards the first line indent marker at the top). Do not begin dragging until you see the double-arrow.

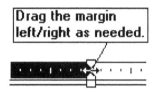

❷ As you drag the margin, a dashed line will appear across the page providing an easy method for aligning the margins.

TIP: *Hold the* **ALT** *key down while dragging a margin marker, to display the margin distances in inches (as shown below) - to adjust the margins more precisely.*

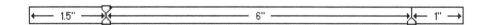

TIP: *If you double-click in the margins on the Ruler Bar, Word will display the "Page Setup" dialog box where you can manually change the settings.*

ADJUSTING THE LINE SPACING

USAGE:

Line spacing is the amount of space between lines of text within a paragraph. When typing a draft, you may want to double space it to allow room for hand-written comments and corrections. Word is set for single line spacing but adjusts the spacing to what is needed to accommodate the largest font size on the line.

The easiest method for adjusting line spacing is through a tool located on the **Home** ribbon:

 Click or tap this tool (within the **Paragraph** section of the Home ribbon) to choose from a list of the most common line spacing settings.

If you select the option in the list (labeled **Line Spacing Options...**), you will be taken to the dialog box displayed on the previous page where you can choose a customized setting.

Use the last two options to quickly add some space before or after the current paragraph.

ADJUSTING PARAGRAPH SPACING

To customize the exact spacing needed before and after each paragraph within a document, you will need to use the **Spacing** section (located on the Layout ribbon) to adjust the spacing between paragraphs.

Click or tap this section to make your changes. Notice you can either enter an actual value in the boxes provided or use the up and down arrows to increase/decrease the current spacing between paragraphs.

For more customization, click or tap the **Paragraph Dialog Box Launcher** (located on the Layout ribbon).

Instructor Note:

Be sure to explain that the first option changes the spacing between lines within a paragraph while the second option adjusts the number of lines before and after a paragraph.

The following dialog box will be displayed:

Select the **Indents and Spacing** tab from the top of the dialog box. The first two sections in this dialog box have nothing to do with line spacing. Instead, look for the third section labeled "Spacing" which is divided into three sets of boxes, as described below:

Before/After   Sets the spacing before and after a paragraph. You can either type a number in the box provided or click on the arrow buttons (located to the right of each box) to increase/decrease the setting.

Line spacing   Sets basic spacing (e.g., single, double).

At   Sets precise spacing for pre-printed forms or documents requiring an exact measurement.

There is also a checkbox within this section that instructs Word not to add a space between paragraphs of the same style.

When done, click or tap on ⌐ OK ⌐.

PARAGRAPH ALIGNMENT

USAGE:

Depending on the type of document you are creating, you may find it preferable to have a report title centered between the left and right margins or to have the paragraphs fully justified.

Word is capable of aligning paragraphs, as shown below:

Left Justified
This paragraph is Left Justified which means that only the left edge is neatly justified.

Center Justification
This paragraph is Center Justified which means that neither the left edge nor the right edge is justified.

Right Justified
This paragraph is Right Justified which means that only the right edge is neatly justified.

Full Justification
This paragraph is Fully Justified which means that both the left edge and the right edge are justified. Only the last line of the paragraph is not justified.

Word is automatically set for left justification.

To change the alignment, place your cursor anywhere within a paragraph and select one of the following tools (located on the **Home** ribbon):

Left Aligned

Centered

Right Aligned

Full Justification

> **TIP:** Typically, the last line of a paragraph is shorter than the rest of the paragraph and may not be justified. To justify the last line, press **SHIFT** + **ENTER** instead of **ENTER** at the end of the line. However, if the line is very short, there may be large gaps between words.

As mentioned previously, you can quickly set the alignment before typing within a blank area by moving your mouse pointer left/right on the page until you see the pointer change to the desired alignment setting.

The mouse pointer will change shape depending on where you move it.

If you double-click in a blank spot when your mouse pointer looks like this, the next item you enter will be left-justified.

If you double-click in a blank spot when your mouse pointer looks like this, Word will automatically indent the first line of new text you enter and left-justify the remainder of the paragraph. This pointer will only appear when your mouse pointer is approximately a half-inch from the left margin.

If you double-click in a blank spot when your mouse pointer looks like this, the next item you enter will be centered.

If you double-click in a blank spot when your mouse pointer looks like this, the next item you enter will be right-justified.

It is also possible to adjust the paragraph alignment through the keyboard, using the following shortcut keys:

CTRL + **J**   (Justified)

CTRL + **E**   (Centered)

CTRL + **R**   (Flush Right)

CTRL + **L**   (Left)

All text from within the current paragraph will be aligned accordingly. As with all other formatting options, you can first select existing text and then alter its alignment.

REVEAL FORMATTING

USAGE:

Word provides a handy feature referred to as **Reveal Formatting**. It can be used to troubleshoot your document when encountering formatting issues, such as font changes and alignment settings.

When activated, this feature reveals all of the formatting properties for the current word or selected text. These properties are displayed within a task pane so that you can quickly modify the format currently being used.

Press SHIFT + F1 to display the Reveal Formatting task pane.

The task pane will change to display the reveal formatting information, as illustrated in the diagram below:

Instructor Note:

This section is important for users creating very complex documents so take your time, explain everything clearly and then allow students some time on their own to practice.

Explain that it is sort of like HTML as far as displaying codes that have been applied to text but may not be seen.

Just like when working with a web page, when things aren't displaying properly, you will need to check out the codes.

The top of the task pane displays a copy of the text (or portion of the text) currently selected. All of the formatting properties that are currently being applied to the selected text will be displayed in the window below the sample.

Simple formatting changes can be applied by accessing the **Selected text** box (located across the top of the Reveal Formatting task pane), as shown below:

Click or tap the down arrow ⏷ (which only appears when you point to the box) to the right of the "Selected text" box to display a list of available options.

Choose from one of the following options:

The first option (labeled **Select All Text with Similar Formatting**) allows you to quickly select other text within the document having the same formatting properties.

The second option (labeled **Apply Formatting of Surrounding Text**) is used to apply the formatting of the text on either side of the current selection. This can be useful if you have inserted a word or phrase within the middle of a paragraph and the inserted text does not match the surrounding format.

The third option (labeled **Clear Formatting**) is used to remove all formatting for the selected text.

The checkbox labeled **Compare to another selection** can be used to quickly see the formatting differences between two pieces of text. To use this option, select the first piece of text, check the box and then select the second piece of text to which the original selection should be compared.

If you then want the second piece of text to match the first, click or tap the down arrow ⏷ (to the right of the "Selected text" box) and choose **Apply Formatting of Original Selection**.

To compare the original selection to a different piece of text, uncheck the box and repeat the process.

Beneath the "Selected text" box you will see different types of formatting, such as font, paragraph and section. Each format (e.g., font, paragraph, section) will have a small triangle beside it which allows you to display or hide the details associated within that format. The number of formats will depend on what is currently selected.

While reviewing the properties of a particular format, you will notice that the properties that can be modified are displayed in blue and underlined (similar to a hyperlink).

⊿ **Font**
  FONT
    (Default) Arial
    12 pt
  LANGUAGE
    English (United States)

Simply click or tap the underlined property to be modified. A dialog box will be displayed where you can make the desired changes.

There are two checkboxes displayed along the bottom of the Reveal Formatting task pane.

If your document contains several styles, use the first checkbox (labeled **Distinguish style source**) to display the style names from which the formatting originates. This allows you to verify the formatting properties that should be applied by a particular style. This option will not be available while comparing the formatting of two selections.

The checkbox labeled **Show all formatting marks** is used to display all of the non-printing symbols, such as hard returns, spaces and tabs within your document. This option is the same as selecting the ¶ tool (located on the **Home** ribbon and discussed previously within this manual).

✗   To remove the Reveal Formatting task pane from view, click or tap the close button (which is located in the upper right corner of the task pane).

CHANGING CASE

USAGE:

Instructor Note:

Everyone loves this feature because we've all accidentally typed a few sentences in all caps before realizing it.

If you have pressed the [CAPS LOCK] key by mistake and continued typing more than a few characters, you can have Word go back and convert the text to the correct case.

Select the text to be converted.

Aa ▾   Click or tap on the **Change Case** tool (located within the Font section on the Home ribbon).

> Sentence case.
>
> lowercase
>
> UPPERCASE
>
> Capitalize Each Word
>
> tOGGLE cASE

The following choices are available within this list:

Sentence case	The first character of each sentence will be capitalized. Word looks for punctuation (a period, exclamation or question mark) to determine the end of a sentence.
lowercase	Converts selected text to all lowercase.
UPPERCASE	Coverts selected text to all uppercase.
Capitalize Each Word	Capitalizes the first letter of each word.
tOGGLE cASE	Switches the case of the selected text to the exact opposite as it is now.

Select the desired case from the list.

INSERTING THE DATE & TIME

USAGE:

You can quickly insert the date and time in the middle of your document. In addition to selecting the exact format for the date/time, you can also specify whether it should be updated automatically. This can be useful for letters you use as a template for new files.

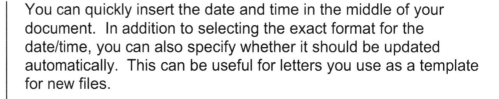 Click or tap on the **Date and Time** tool (located within the Text section on the Insert ribbon).

The following dialog box will be displayed:

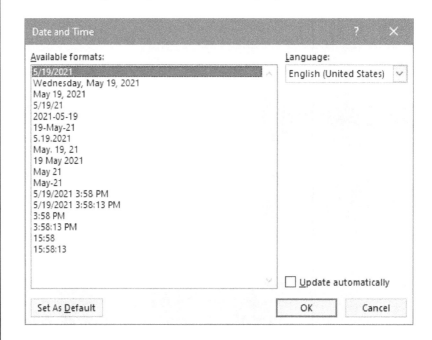

Click or tap on the Set As Default button to change the default setting within Word to the currently selected format. This setting will be used for any date codes (e.g., when working with headers or footers) added to this or future documents.

Select the desired format and choose OK .

PRACTICE EXERCISE

Instructions:	❶	Open the document **AUDIT**.
	❷	Insert the date and time at the top and set these margins: Top - **2.5"** Bottom - **1"** Left - **1.5"** Right - **1.5"**
	❸	Justification should be set to **FULL** for the file.
	❹	Change the attributes (as shown) and the color of the address section.
	❺	Using the highlighter pen, emphasize the sentence reading, "What could have been a simple matter..."
	❻	When you are done, save and print (or preview).

Mr. John Doe
Sanderson Accounting Firm
111 West 57th Street, Suite 1500
New York, NY 10014

Dear Mr. Doe,

*I am writing on behalf of my company to let you know that we will **no longer** be doing business with your firm.*

*Because of your **inexperience** in the matter along with messy record-keeping on our part, we failed to provide the necessary paperwork needed to pass the audit.*

What could have been a simple matter has now turned into an accounting nightmare. Your firm is largely responsible for that outcome.

Although I realize there was no malice intended on your part, I want you to know that we will not be continuing our working relationship with your firm.

Sincerely,

Sally Smith
Vice President of Operations

PRACTICE EXERCISE

Instructions:	❶	Open the document you created at the beginning of the class to make the following modifications:
		Top Margin - **2"** Line Spacing - **2** (for the first paragraph only!) Justification - **Full** (for the entire document)
	❷	Be sure to make the attribute and line spacing changes shown.
	❸	When you are done, save and print (or preview).

TO ALL EMPLOYEES:

As our fiscal year comes to a close later this month, we ask that each employee keep their overtime hours down to a minimum.

*At the moment, our company is on-target to meet its projected earnings estimates but we need the assistance of all of our employees to keep costs down. Since overtime is one of our most costly expenditures we incur, we especially want to ask **supervisors** in each division to keep overtime hours down.*

Thank you in advance for your cooperation.

PRACTICE EXERCISE

Instructions:	❶	Open the document **AUDIT** to remove all of the formatting attributes placed in the file during one of the last exercises. Be sure to reset <u>all</u> formatting including margins and justification.
	❷	Be sure to save and print (or preview).

Mr. John Doe
Sanderson Accounting Firm
111 West 57th Street, Suite 1500
New York, NY 10014

Dear Mr. Doe,

I am writing on behalf of my company to let you know that we will no longer be doing business with your firm.

Because of your inexperience in the matter along with messy record-keeping on our part, we failed to provide the necessary paperwork needed to pass the audit.

What could have been a simple matter has now turned into an accounting nightmare. Your firm is largely responsible for that outcome.

Although I realize there was no malice intended on your part, I want you to know that we will not be continuing our working relationship with your firm.

Sincerely,

Sally Smith
Vice President of Operations

Module Four

- **Setting Tabs**
- **Indenting vs. Tabs**
- **Inserting Page Breaks**
- **Adding Blank Pages**
- **Creating Cover Pages**

SETTING TABS

USAGE:

Tabs are used for creating columnar lists of numbers and text. As with other paragraph settings, tabs affect the current paragraph and are stored in the paragraph marker. These settings are then duplicated for the next paragraph when you press ENTER. The default tab stops appear every half inch.

When creating tabs, Word allows you to create five types: Left, Center, Right, Decimal, and Bar.

The left edge of the ruler contains an icon  used to select the type of tab or indent required.

⌊	Left Tab	Text is left-aligned under the tab.
⊥	Center Tab	Text is centered under the tab.
⌋	Right Tab	Text is right-aligned under the tab.
⊥	Decimal Tab	This is used for numerical data. The decimal point in the value (number) lines up under the tab.
⌶	Bar Tab	Adds a vertical bar (|) at the tab stop before the text. This can be useful for creating a faux column separator.
▽	First Line Indent	Adjusts the indent of the first line of a paragraph.
△	Hanging Indent	Adjusts the rest of the paragraph (the body), allowing you to create hanging indents.

Instructor Note:

This module should begin after a break so students are somewhat fresh.

In a blank document, have them select each type of tab and then type in a word or number to see it in action.

To set a tab, follow the steps outlined below:

❶ Choose the appropriate tab style and then move to the position on the ruler where the tab should be inserted.

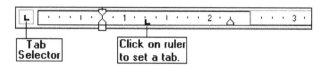

❷ Click or tap in the lower half of the ruler at the desired location and the tab will appear on the ruler.

REMOVING TABS FROM THE RULER

Grab the tab stop and pull it down off the ruler.

MOVING A TAB STOP POSITION

Grab the tab stop and drag it to the new location. A dashed vertical line will appear to help guide you.

CREATING DOT LEADER TABS

You can use dot leaders for your tabs for items such as phone lists, table of contents, and indexes.

Chapter 1..1
Chapter 2..9

To set a dot leader tab or to set several tabs at once, point to the location on the ruler where you want to set the new tab and then double-click or double-tap on that blank spot (towards the lower portion of the ruler).

You can also access the Tabs dialog box by switching to the **Layout** ribbon and launching the **Paragraph** dialog box. From within the dialog box, click or tap the Tabs... button.

The following dialog box will be displayed:

To clear all existing tabs so that you can start setting new tabs, click or tap the Clear All button.

If you need to remove a single existing tab, highlight it from within the list and then click or tap Clear .

To set a new tab, type in the position number, set the alignment type, a leader style and then click or tap the Set button.

When done setting all tabs, choose OK .

PRACTICE EXERCISE

Instructions:	❶	Create two tab definitions.
	❷	The first definition will consist of two centered tabs for the second and third column headings.
	❸	Once those tabs have been set, enter the information for the column headings.
	❹	Your next step will be to set the second set which will consist of only two tabs (a decimal tab and a right tab) for the actual data.
	❺	Enter the remainder of the information as shown below.
	❻	Be sure to save and print (or preview) the file.

<u>Employee</u>	<u>Rate</u>	<u>Salary</u>
Willy Wilson	$39.75	$4,500
Sally Smith	52.30	6,400
Buster Brown	49.00	5,100
David Davidson	15.50	950
Joe Doe	55.00	7,800
Jill Jillian	74.50	9,100
Milton Miller	52.50	6,350

INDENTING PARAGRAPHS

USAGE:

Should you want to change the left margin for only one paragraph, you may find using the indent command easier than changing the left margin. Word actually allows for three indent settings: left, right and first line.

The **left indent** controls the left edge of all lines within a paragraph except the first. This indent is measured from the left margin. A paragraph's **right indent** controls the right edge of all lines in the paragraph. This indent is measured from the right margin. A paragraph's **first line indent** controls only the left edge of the paragraph's first line. This indent is measured from the left margin. Setting it to a negative number would create a "hanging indent."

 Click or tap this tool (located within the Paragraph section on the Home Ribbon) as many times as needed to **indent** a paragraph.

 Click or tap this tool to **outdent** a paragraph.

 To enter a more precise value, use these two boxes (located in Paragraph section of the Layout Ribbon) for the indent/outdent.

Instructor Note:

When trying to create tabs or change margins, users often pull the indent marker by mistake so take your time and explain its purpose and allow students to play around and see what happens when they move it.

When using the ruler to set indents, drag the indent marker to the desired position. Notice that when you drag the left indent marker, the first line marker moves with it. This keeps the first line indentation you set as you change the left indent. It is possible to move the first line marker separately.

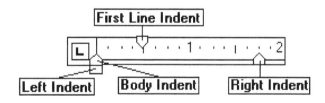

CREATING A HANGING INDENT

Hold [SHIFT] down while dragging the left indent marker on the ruler. You can also change the tab selector to the hanging indent symbol ▽ and then click or tap on the ruler to set the indent.

ADDING MANUAL PAGE BREAKS

USAGE:

Although Word automatically paginates your documents using the margins and paper size settings as its guide, there will be times when you will want to add a page break manually.

To add a page break to your document, move your cursor to the location where the current page should end.

Click or tap on the **Page Break** tool (located within the Pages section on the Insert ribbon).

Page Break

If you prefer using the keyboard, press CTRL + ENTER

REMOVING A PAGE BREAK

If you place a page break in your document manually, it is possible to remove it yourself.

Turn on **paragraph markers** ¶ (from the Paragraph section on the Home ribbon).

Manual page breaks are displayed as thin dotted lines with the words "Page Break" in the middle.

¶

············Page Break············¶

Place your cursor at the beginning of the Page Break line to be removed and press DEL.

INSERTING BLANK PAGES

USAGE:

Although Word automatically paginates your documents using the margins and paper size settings as its guide, there might be a time when you want to have a blank page inserted in the middle of your document.

This can be useful when creating long documents with several sections. You might decide that a blank page between sections makes sense, such as before a new chapter.

To add a blank page to your document, move your cursor to the location where the current page should end and the blank page should be inserted.

Click or tap the **Blank Page** tool (located within the Pages section on the Insert ribbon).

A new blank page will have been inserted into your document at the current cursor location.

> **TIP:** You can quickly insert a blank page by pressing
> [CTRL] + [ENTER] *twice.*

CREATING COVER PAGES

USAGE:

Word has a feature that allows you to add custom cover pages for a more polished feel to your document. You first select one of the predefined cover pages that Word includes and then you edit it to include your own text.

To add a cover page to the current document, follow these steps:

❶ ▢ **Cover Page ▾**   Click or tap the **Cover Page** tool (located within the Pages section on the Insert ribbon).

❷ 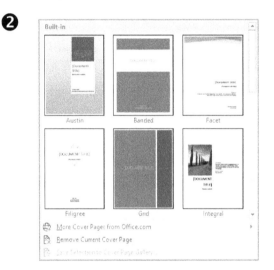 From the pull-down list of built-in cover pages, select the one you'd like to insert into your document.

Notice there is an option within this pull-down list to remove the current cover page – in case you change your mind after inserting one.

Instructor Note:

If time permits, give students some time to play with this since they maybe won't use it often but it is quite useful for submitting business quotes, resumes, presentations, etc.

By default, the cover page will be placed at the beginning of the document.

If you right-click on one of the built-in cover page templates, you will be provided with additional options for inserting the cover page.

Once the cover page has been inserted, simply click in each of the predefined sections (Document title, etc.) to customize the text.

The last option within the pull-down list can be used to save your own custom cover page to the Cover Page Gallery. You must first select the page you want to save and then choose **Save Selection to Cover Page Gallery**.

PRACTICE EXERCISE

Instructions:	❶	Open the document **ENERGY PLAN** and make the changes as shown below so that the document contains centered text and indented paragraphs.
	❷	Insert a cover page – whichever you want and then edit the text to be appropriate with the subject matter.
	❸	Be sure to save and print (or preview) the revised document.

COMPANY ENERGY-SAVINGS PLAN

1. Have all employees turn off their computers and monitors at the end of each working day.

2. Install energy-efficient lighting in all departments.

3. Encourage ride-sharing by offering monthly bonuses to employees who sign up to ride the company van at least two days per week.

4. Organize weekly lunch barbeques onsite to save employees from driving during their lunch hours.

5. Purchase electric vans for company carpooling.

6. Set thermostat to 68 degrees during winter months (to save heat) and 78 degrees during summer months (to save air).

Module Five

- **Moving Text**
- **Copying Text**
- **Dragging & Dropping**
- **The Office Clipboard**
- **Working with the Thesaurus**
- **The Grammar Checker**
- **Smart Lookup**
- **Using Bookmarks**
- **Printing Envelopes**

MOVING TEXT

USAGE:

If you have typed a document and then decide that a portion of the text should be placed in a different area in the file, you can move the contents by cutting and pasting.

When you choose to cut text, Word removes it from the current document and places it in the Windows Clipboard (a temporary storage area).

Only the last item that was cut or copied is stored within the clipboard.

To move a block of text from one location to another within your document, follow these steps:

❶ Select the portion of the document to be moved.

❷ ✂ Cut   Click or tap on the **Cut** tool (which is located on the Home ribbon). The block of text is temporarily removed from the screen and placed in the clipboard.

❸ Move your cursor to the new location.

❹   Click or tap the **Paste** tool.
Paste

> **TIP:**   Using the keyboard, press *CTRL*+*X* to **Cut** the selected text and *CTRL*+*V* to **Paste** the text.

PASTE FORMAT OPTIONS

Once an item has been pasted, a small clipboard icon is displayed at that location within the document.

Click or tap this icon to select from a list of options that defines how the item should be pasted. These options depend on the type of content you are pasting, the application you are pasting from and the format of the text where you are pasting.

When you click or tap the clipboard icon from within your document, a pull-down list appears offering several formatting options.

Choose from one of the following options:

 Select this option to retain the original format of the pasted item.

 Choose this option to merge the original format of the copied text with the format of where you're pasting it. For example, if the original text was bold and the location where you're inserting the text is underlined, this option will paste the text with both the bold and underline formats applied.

 Select this option to paste the clipboard contents as a graphic image. If the clipboard contains text, you will not be able to edit the pasted image even though it looks like regular text.

 Select this option to paste the text without any format. For example, if the original text was bold, the pasted text will no longer be bold.

NOTE:	The number of available icons will vary depending on the type of item being pasted.

Set Default Paste   Choose this option to access a dialog box where you can set the default format options for pasting future items within your document.

COPYING TEXT

USAGE:

If you need a portion of text copied within the same file or placed in another document within Word, you can copy the text. This leaves the text in its original location while taking a copy of it to the new location.

To copy a block of text from one location to another within the document, follow these steps

❶ Select the portion of the document to be copied using either the mouse or the keyboard.

❷ ⎙ Copy   Click or tap the **Copy** tool (which is located on the Home ribbon). The block of text is temporarily copied to the clipboard.

❸ Move your cursor to the new location.

❹ Paste   Click or tap the **Paste** tool.

> **TIP:**   Using the keyboard, press [CTRL]+[C] to **Copy** text and [CTRL]+[V] to **Paste**.

> **Instructor Note:**
>
> *If you're using our example, have students select the last sentence in the first paragraph, "**Since overtime is…**" and copy it to the end of the second paragraph so that it appears in both places.*

DRAGGING & DROPPING

USAGE:

Word also allows you to cut/copy and paste text within a document by using the **Drag & Drop** feature available in most Windows programs. This feature allows mouse users to place the pointer in the middle of selected text and "drag" the block to a new location. Once the location is reached, you "drop" the selected text off.

MOVING TEXT WITH DRAG & DROP

❶ Begin by selecting the text to be moved.

❷ Place the mouse pointer in the middle of the selected text. The pointer should change to an arrow.

❸ Begin dragging the block of text. A small piece of paper moves with you. Notice a light cursor also appears - indicating where the text will be placed when the mouse button is released.

❹ When you reach the correct location, release the mouse button. The selected text should have been moved.

COPYING TEXT WITH DRAG & DROP

❶ Begin by selecting the text to be copied.

❷ Place the mouse pointer in the middle of the selected text. The pointer should change to an arrow.

❸ While holding the [CTRL] key down, drag the block of text. A small piece of paper with a plus sign moves with you. Notice a light cursor - indicating where the text will be placed when you release the mouse button.

❹ When you reach the correct spot, release the mouse button.

Instructor Note:

Students sometimes move or copy and item by mistake – they are trying to highlight but then begin dragging. Mention that and show them how easy it is to do.

USING THE OFFICE CLIPBOARD

USAGE:

You can use the Office Clipboard to collect multiple items (both text and graphics) to be pasted within Word or other Office 365 applications. The standard Windows clipboard is only able to store one item at a time.   You have to paste whatever you have cut or copied before your next cut/copy can be completed.

However, the Office Clipboard can store up to 24 items at a time, making it easy to collect multiple items to be pasted. If you copy a 25th item, the first item in your clipboard will automatically be removed to make room for the latest entry.

Depending on your computer's settings, choosing to copy an item and then copying a second one without pasting the first may trigger the Clipboard task pane to be displayed.

If the task pane is not automatically displayed, you can manually display it by accessing the following tool:

Click or tap the **Clipboard Task Pane Launcher** ⌐ (located along the left side of the Home ribbon).

The Office Clipboard will automatically be opened and placed within a task pane, as shown below:

The clipboard will display each of the cut or copied items - with the latest item placed at the top of the list.

If you have cut or copied several entries, a scroll bar will be placed along the right side so that you can quickly move through the items.

A small icon is placed to the left of each object to indicate what application the cut or copied item was originally created in.

Move to the location to which the item(s) should be pasted.

Click or tap the clipboard item to be pasted.

There are two tools available across the top of the clipboard:

Click or tap this tool to paste each of the items stored within the Office Clipboard in the current document (or within the current Office application).

Click or tap this button to clear the contents of the Office Clipboard. It will also clear the Windows Clipboard.

To remove a single item from the clipboard, point to the item you want to remove until you see a small down arrow ⏷.

Click or tap the down arrow ⏷ and select **Delete** from the list of options.

CLIPBOARD OPTIONS

Towards the bottom of the clipboard is a button ⌷Options⌷ which is used to change the display settings for the Office Clipboard.

> Show Office Clipboard Automatically
>
> Show Office Clipboard When Ctrl+C Pressed Twice
>
> Collect Without Showing Office Clipboard
>
> ✓ Show Office Clipboard Icon on Taskbar
>
> ✓ Show Status Near Taskbar When Copying

Instructor Note:

Go over each of these options.

From the five options available, check the box labeled **Show Office Clipboard Automatically** to open the clipboard within the task pane when two items in a row have been copied.

Select **Show Office Clipboard When Ctrl+C Pressed Twice** to display the Office Clipboard after pressing the copy shortcut keys.

Choose **Collect Without Showing Office Clipboard** if you prefer not to display the clipboard within the task pane when two items in a row have been copied. This option displays the clipboard icon on the taskbar even if you are in a different application. Make sure the first two options have not been checked.

Select **Show Office Clipboard Icon on Taskbar** to display the clipboard icon at the bottom of your screen.

Choose **Show Status Near Taskbar When Copying** to display the status of a copied item on the taskbar.

Check each of the options you would like to enable from the list. Click a second time to disable the option.

Once the Office Clipboard has been activated, an icon will be placed on the Windows taskbar (notification tray) along the bottom right of your screen.

If you don't see the Office Clipboard icon on your taskbar, it may be one of the hidden items. Click on ︿ to view the hidden items.

If you right-click or tap and hold (if using a touch screen) on the clipboard icon located along the taskbar at the bottom of your screen, the following list of options will be displayed:

From this list, you can choose to display the Office Clipboard, clear all of the items currently being stored within the clipboard, or close the clipboard. The last item within this list allows you to specify the display options for the clipboard (which were discussed on the previous page).

If you do not specify otherwise, the collected items remain in the Clipboard until you close all Office applications.

PRACTICE EXERCISE

Instructions:	❶	Open the document **ENERGY PLAN**.
	❷	Move the paragraphs in the order shown below.
		Hint: You may want to renumber the paragraphs **before** moving them.
	❸	Be sure to save and print (or preview) the file.

COMPANY ENERGY-SAVINGS PLAN

1. Purchase electric vans for company carpooling.

2. Encourage ride-sharing by offering monthly bonuses to employees who sign up to ride the company van at least two days per week.

3. Set thermostat to 68 degrees during winter months (to save heat) and 78 degrees during summer months (to save air).

4. Install energy-efficient lighting in all departments.

5. Have all employees turn off their computers and monitors at the end of each working day.

6. Organize weekly lunch barbeques onsite to save employees from driving during their lunch hours.

COMPANY ENERGY-SAVINGS PLAN

WORKING WITH THE THESAURUS

USAGE:

If you have used a word several times within the same paragraph, you may want to use the thesaurus to look up an alternative word. You can also use this feature to find a word similar in meaning to the one you want to use but gets the point across a bit stronger.

Thesaurus

Select the word you want to look up and then switch to the Review ribbon and click or tap on this tool (located within the Proofing section) to activate the Thesaurus.

> **Instructor Note:**
>
> *Have the class choose a word together to begin this section.*
>
> *After you've discussed all of the options, have them look a word or two up on their own for practice.*

A listing of words similar to the one currently selected will be provided within the task pane. If there is more than a screenful, you can move through the list by using the scroll bars provided.

Notice if the selected word has more than one meaning, Word displays each of those meanings with a list of alternative words. Each different meaning will have a small triangle to the left, which allows you to display or hide its set of alternative words. The number of meanings will depend on what word is currently selected.

Towards the bottom of the Thesaurus pane is a small section that allows you to hear the pronunciation of a word by selecting the word and then clicking on the  icon.

Beneath the speaker icon is a definition of the selected word.

NOTE:	*You must be signed in to your Microsoft account in order to see definitions.*

REPLACING A WORD

To replace the word in your document with one of the choices provided within the task pane, simply click or tap on the down arrow ⏷ beside the new word and choose **Insert** from the list.

Notice you can also copy the word to paste in another location or lookup the selected word.

LOOKING UP A NEW WORD

To look up a different word, simply click or tap in the box labeled **Search** and then enter the new word. After entering the word, either press ENTER or click on ⌕

If you have looked up more than one word, click or tap on the small back arrow (**<**) to return to the previous listing.

USING THE AUTO GRAMMAR CHECKER

USAGE:

Word not only offers a spell checker but can also act as a proofreader - letting you know of any grammatical errors within your document. While spelling errors are underlined in red, grammatical errors are flagged using a double blue underline. This underline is for viewing purposes only and will not be printed.

Once a sentence is flagged as having a possible mistake, you will notice that the status bar at the bottom of the screen displays an **X** with the **Proofing** icon ▢ꭓ. This indicates that a spelling or grammatical error has been found in your document.

You do not need to access the grammar checking box to correct the mistake. Instead, you can use your mouse, as outlined below:

Point to the underlined word or phrase and click your **[RIGHT]** mouse button once.

A pop-up menu will be displayed:

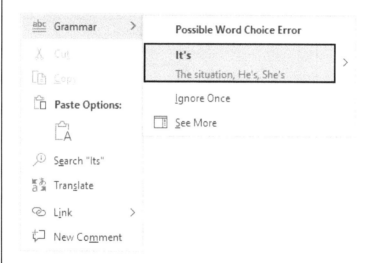

Notice that **Grammar** has already been selected (along the top, left side of the pop-up menu). The top portion of this pop-up (along the right side) offers suggestions for the possible mistake.

Notice that Word allows you to **ignore** the flagged text if you want to keep it as is.

You can also choose to access the Editor panel (shown on the next page) by selecting **See More**.

THE GRAMMAR CHECKER

USAGE:

Before printing and sending a document out for others to read, you should always check it for grammatical errors as well as spelling mistakes you may have made.

 Click or tap the **Editor** tool (located within the Proofing section on the Review ribbon).

Word will open the Editor panel and display an overview of the spelling and grammatical issues it finds within your document:

The top section of the Editor panel includes a button showing the total number of results (possible errors) within your document. Click/tap on this button to cycle through all the possible errors Word has flagged.

In the **Corrections** section, you will see the number of spelling and/or grammatical errors that have been flagged. Click on the Grammar option.

Word displays the flagged word and its surrounding text:

Click on ◁» to hear the error out loud.

Below the error, Word lists suggestions to correct the flagged sentence. If one of the suggestions is correct, click or tap on the suggestion.

Click on the down arrow beside a suggested correction to have Word read the sentence out loud or have it spelled out loud.

If you want to keep the existing spelling, select **Ignore Once**. If the flagged text is used throughout the file and you want to keep it as is, you can then choose **Don't check for this issue**.

Choose **Settings** to access the advanced grammar settings.

✕   Click or tap this button to remove the panel from the screen. After running the grammar checker, be sure to save your document again.

SMART SEARCH

USAGE:

Microsoft has a **Search** feature that allows you to fact-check or learn more about terms or phrases you are using in your document.

When you use the Search feature, Word opens the Insights panel, powered by Microsoft Bing. This panel offers more than just definitions. If you have selected a person's name, the Insights panel will display biographical information on that person and links to articles related to them.

When you select a word or phrase, right-click it, and choose **Search** from the context menu, the insights panel will be opened, providing definitions, Wiki articles, and top related searches from across the web.

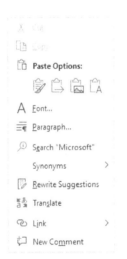

Point to the term or phrase you want to look up and then click your **[RIGHT]** mouse button once or tap and hold (if using a touch screen).

From the pop-up menu, choose ***Search***.

NOTE:	*You can also display the Smart Lookup panel through the ribbon by selecting **References → Search** and then entering the term/phrase/name you'd like to learn more about.*

Instructor Note:

Have the class enter the first term/phrase together and then (if time allows) let them try it on their own.

The highlighted term or phrase will be sent to Bing and the **Insights** panel will be displayed along the right side of the screen:

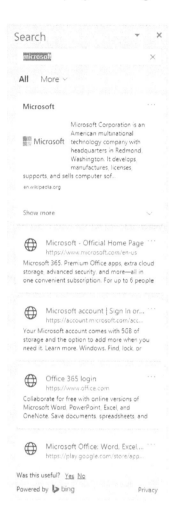

There are two options across the top of the Insights panel:

All This section shows all articles and web content on the phrase/term/name being searched.

More Use this option to display only the articles, media or help information.

When you are done reading content on the phrase you searched for, click on the **X** button (along the top of the Insights panel) to close it.

USING BOOKMARKS

USAGE:

A "Bookmark" in Word is similar to a physical bookmark you might use when reading a book - if you want to return to the page you left off, you insert a bookmark at that location.

By default, Word remembers the last page you were working on when you previously closed the document. If you get interrupted while working on a document, this allows you to quickly pick up where you left off.

You can also use bookmarks to mark different sections of a large document. Instead of trying to remember what page the section was in, you could simply go to the bookmark.

Word allows you to set several bookmarks within a document. Each bookmark is given a unique name so that you can quickly move to a particular location. The name you assign to the bookmark should remind you of why you set that bookmark.

CREATING BOOKMARKS

Bookmark

Place your cursor at the location you want to mark and then click or tap on the **Bookmark** tool (located within the Links section on the Insert ribbon).

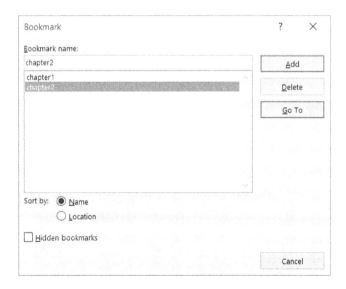

You may now enter a name for the bookmark (up to 40 characters - no spaces) and then click or tap the [Add] button.

GOING TO A BOOKMARK

To quickly go to one of your bookmarks, press **CTRL** + **G**

The following box will be displayed asking where you want to go:

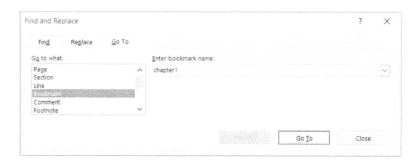

Be sure to select **Bookmark** from the section labeled "Go to what" and then choose your bookmark from the list provided (in the pull-down list along the right side of the dialog box).

After selecting the bookmark, click or tap Go To . Your cursor will be taken to the location where the bookmark was originally created.

The box remains on the screen until you choose Close .

DELETING A BOOKMARK

If you no longer use or need a bookmark, you should delete it from the document to remove excess codes.

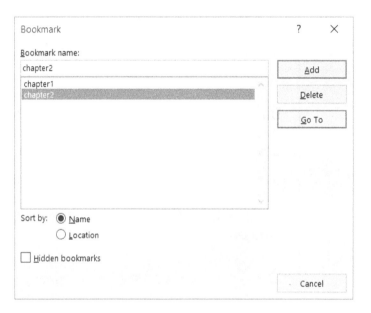
Click or tap the **Bookmark** tool (located within the Links section on the Insert ribbon).

The following dialog box will be displayed:

From the list of bookmarks, select the bookmark to be removed and click or tap Delete .

PRACTICE EXERCISE

Instructions:	❶	Open the document **POLICY**
	❷	Add the following bookmarks:
		Purpose at the beginning of the first section labeled "PURPOSE".
		Sickness at the beginning of the second section labeled "SICKNESS".
		Accidents at the beginning of the fourth section labeled "ACCIDENTS".
	❸	Practice moving from bookmark to bookmark within the document.
	❹	Using the thesaurus, find an alternative word for **Ideally** in the second paragraph of section 4.
	❺	Run the grammar checker and correct any mistakes you feel should be made to the file.
	❻	Save and close the document.

PRINTING ENVELOPES

USAGE:

Envelopes are a major part of word processing. In the past, placing return and mailing addresses on envelopes ranged from using a typewriter to print labels and sticking them on envelopes to simply handwriting them. Word has an enhanced feature that can automatically capture the mailing address from the current document and place it on an envelope.

The return address can also be filled in or left off, depending on whether you are using preprinted envelopes.

Once you have completed typing your letter, you will be ready to add an envelope.

✉ Envelopes — Click or tap the **Envelope** tool (located within the Create section on the Mailings ribbon).

The following dialog box will be displayed:

If needed, select the tab labeled **Envelopes**. If you are using Outlook, click on ⊞ ▾ in the Delivery and/or Return address section of this dialog box to choose from a list of stored addresses. Notice there is a checkbox to **omit** the return address if you are using pre-printed envelopes.

If everything is correct, select [Print] to immediately begin printing the envelope.

If you are not ready to print, click or tap on [Add to Document] to add the envelope to the beginning of the document. The envelope will be added to a page numbered 0.

☐ Add electronic postage   If you have an electronic postage application installed (such as stamps.com), you can check this box to instruct Word to automatically print the postage on the envelope.

Click or tap [E-postage Properties...] to customize your electronic postage settings.

ENVELOPE OPTIONS

To change the size of the envelope, add bar codes, or change the fonts for the envelope, select the  Options... button. A second dialog box will be displayed, as shown below:

Envelope size	Click or tap the down arrow ⌄ beside this option to choose from a list of predefined sizes.
Delivery address	Use this section to define the font and placement of the delivery address.
Return address	Use this section to define the font and placement of the return address.

A preview is provided along the bottom of this dialog box.

PRINTING OPTIONS

Select the second tab (labeled **Printing Options**) to change how the envelope will be fed into the printer and from which paper tray.

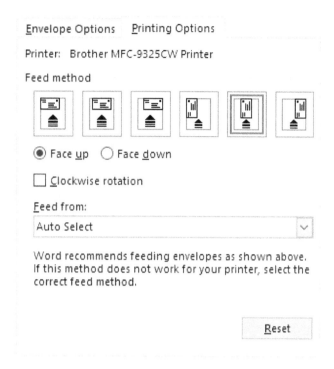

Feed method	Select the way in which the envelope will be fed into the printer. You will also need to include whether the envelope should be fed face up or face down.
Clockwise rotation	When feeding envelopes vertically, check this box to reverse the actual printing direction.
Feed from	Click or tap the down arrow ⌄ beside this option to define how the envelopes will be fed into the printer (through a specific printer tray or manually).

When done, click or tap [OK] .

If You Have Time

- **Mailing Labels**
- **Working with Templates**
- **Document Themes**

MAILING LABELS

USAGE:

Instructor Note:

This is another item that students really want to know about.

Have them create a page of return address labels.

Word is commonly used to produce mailing labels. This process is as simple as providing the program with the information it needs to know about your labels (printer type, label type/size, quantity).

You can print an address on a single mailing label or print the same address on every label on an entire sheet of mailing labels.

You can either specify the mailing address and return address from the one contained in the current document or you can enter the address while in the labels dialog box.

Select the **Labels** tool (located within the Create section on the Mailings ribbon).

The following dialog box will be displayed:

Be sure to select the **Labels** tab from the top of the dialog box.

If working with a document containing a mailing address, Word will select it as the text for the labels. Click or tap ⊞ ▼ in the Address section of this box to choose from a list of stored addresses.

To print multiple return addresses, check **Use return address**.

In the bottom left corner of the dialog box are options to print a **Full Page of the same label** or a **Single label**. If you are not printing a full page of labels, select the **Single label** option, which allows you to specify the number of labels to print.

To begin printing your labels, click or tap the ⸢ Print ⸣ button.

CHANGING LABEL FORMATS

Word has all of the standard Avery label definitions available as well as many other label vendors.

To choose a different label format, select Options... .

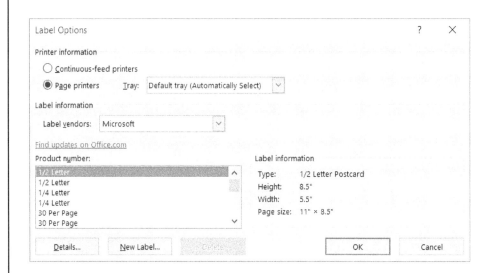

Select the type of printer on which the labels will be printed.

Choose between continuous-feed and page printer label formats, depending on your requirements.

Select the vendor of the labels you are using.

Next, choose the type of label from the **Product number** section. To the right of the product number is a "Label information" box which displays details for the currently selected product to help you determine the correct label to use.

CREATING CUSTOM LABELS

If you have labels that do not fit any of the predefined formats, choose the format closest to your label and click or tap New Label... .

The following window will be displayed:

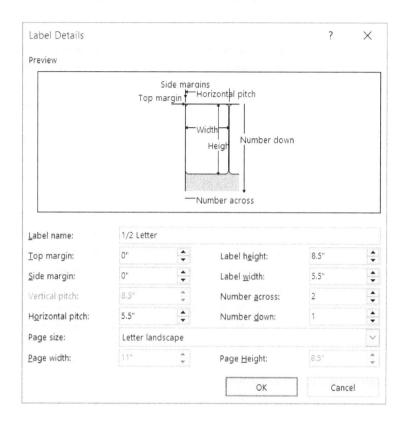

Change the **Label** name to identify your custom label.

Next, change the format features as needed for your custom label.

As you make your changes, Word adjusts the **Preview** of the label to match your specifications.

When all changes have been made, click or tap OK .

TEMPLATES

USAGE:

Word's **Template** feature allows you to create documents which may be used for files with standard information or formatting codes. Rather than creating new documents each time, a template file may be set up.

Templates may consist of text, styles and/or formatting codes. There are several built-in templates to create memos, fax covers, newsletters, and other business as well as personal documents.

When you create a new document, Word needs to know which template to apply to the new file. The default setting is a template called **Normal**. If you do not tell Word otherwise, all new documents will be based on this template.

The "Normal" template is a blank document containing the default margin, character and paragraph formatting codes. You may edit the "Normal" template or create a number of your own templates. Template files within Word contain the extension **.DOTX**

Once the template is saved, you can create new documents based on that template. However, Word needs to know what folder your personal templates will be stored in before you can create a new document based on your templates.

DEFINING YOUR TEMPLATE FOLDER

To define the location of your templates, follow these steps:

Select **Options** from the pull-down list of items within the File tab on the ribbon.

❷ Select the **SAVE** option (along the left).

The following window will be displayed:

❸ By default, Word stores templates in a folder labeled Custom Office Templates. If for some reason you need to change the default location, click or tap in the box labeled **Default personal templates location** and enter a new location (drive and folder) where you will be storing your templates.

> **NOTE:** *Since there's unfortunately no* Browse... *button in this box to search your system for the folder, you'll need to know the exact path yourself.*
>
> *A solution could be clicking or tapping the* Browse... *button on the box above, locate the path and then copy and paste it in this box.*

❹ When done, click or tap OK .

CREATING A NEW TEMPLATE

The simplest method for defining a new template is to create a document as you would any other and then save it as a template.

After creating the document and inserting all of the necessary codes and graphics for the template, follow the steps outlined below to save it as a template for future documents to be based on.

❶   Select **Save As** from the pull-down list of options within the File tab on the ribbon.

The following window will be displayed:

❷ Click on 📂 Browse. From the next window (shown below), click or tap on the down arrow ∨ beside the **Save as type** option and select "Word Template (*.dotx)".

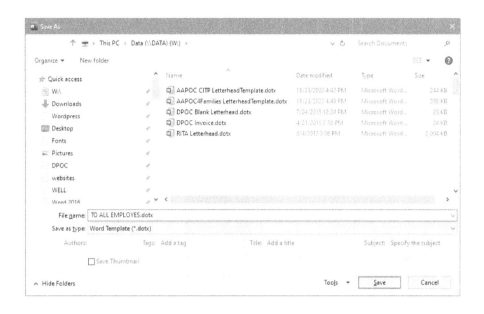

❸ Be sure you have entered a descriptive name for the template before clicking or tapping the ⎍Save⎍ button.

NOTE:	Notice that Word automatically assigns the extension *.DOTX* to template files.
	Normal Microsoft Word documents are assigned the extension *.DOCX*.

USING A TEMPLATE

To use the template that you created, you will follow the usual steps to create a new document with one exception. You will choose your template as the one to base the new document on.

To create a new document based on an existing template, follow the steps outlined below.

❶ Select **New** from the pull-down list of options within the File tab on the ribbon.

Instructor Note:

Have students start off in a blank document, create a template with a cover page and various titles/fonts, save the template and then create a new document based on their template.

The following window will be displayed:

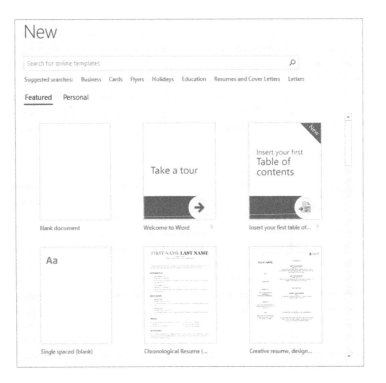

Instructor Note:

Point out that "Featured" and "Personal" only appear after you have created and stored a personal template.

❷ Notice that Word automatically displays the Featured templates (those created by Microsoft). Select Personal (from the top of the window) as the type of templates to be displayed.

❸ Word will change to display your personal templates. Select the one you want to use by double-clicking or double-tapping on it.

A new document will be created – using the formatting defined in the selected template.

Instructor Note:

Be sure to take students through editing their just-saved template so they see how to find it. Point out the different file extension.

EDITING A TEMPLATE

If you realize that a template needs to be modified, you can open it as you would any other document.

Once opened, you will be able to edit the template and then save it again. You can also edit the **Normal** template to set any defaults you would like applied to all documents created using the default template.

NOTE:	Don't forget that Word automatically assigns the extension **.DOTX** to template files so your template will be stored under .DOTX file types rather than the usual .DOCX.

APPLYING A DOCUMENT THEME

USAGE:

You can quickly and easily format an entire document to give it a professional and modern look by applying a document theme.

A document theme is a set of formatting choices that include a set of theme colors, a set of theme fonts (including heading and body text fonts), and a set of theme effects (lines and fill effects).

To quickly apply one of the existing document themes to the current file, click or tap the **Themes** tool (within the Document Formatting section on the Design ribbon).

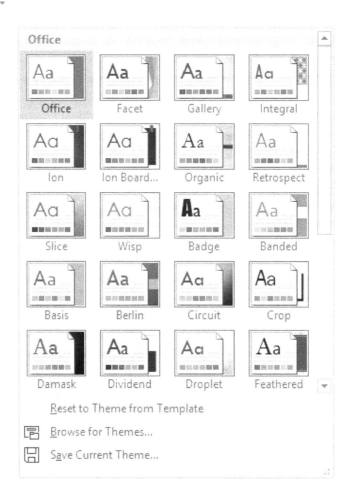

Select the theme to be applied from the list provided. If you decide you don't like the theme you selected, notice there is an option to reset the theme back to the original template setting. You can also make changes to the theme and then save it as a new theme.

Colors

Click or tap this button (located within the **Document Formatting** section of the Design ribbon) to customize the theme colors being applied to your document.

A list of theme colors will be displayed. Click or tap on the one you want to apply. Notice you can also choose to create your own color theme.

A

Fonts

Click or tap this tool (located within the **Document Formatting** section of the Design ribbon) to customize the theme fonts being applied to your document.

A pull-down list of theme fonts will be displayed. Click or tap on the one you want to apply to your document. Notice you can also create new theme fonts.

 Paragraph Spacing ▾

Click or tap on this tool (located within the **Document Formatting** section of the Design ribbon) to customize the paragraph spacing for this theme.

 Effects ▾

Click or tap on this tool (located within the **Document Formatting** section of the Design ribbon) to customize the theme effects being applied to your document.

A pull-down list of theme effects will be displayed. Click or tap the one you want to apply.

⊘ Set as Default

Use this tool to save your current theme settings so that they will be used for any new blank document you create.

CHANGING THE PAGE COLOR

USAGE:

You can quickly and easily change the color of a page to make it appear more professional. This can also be useful if you'd like the document to stand out a bit but don't have color paper on which to print it.

To quickly change the background color of the page, click or tap this tool (located within the **Page Background** section on the Design ribbon).

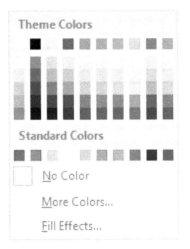

From the list provided, select the color you wish to apply. Notice as you scroll through the options, Word offers a preview of the page color for you to see before making your choice.

PRACTICE EXERCISE

Instructions:		
	❶	Create a **professional** letter using one of the available templates. Fill in the recipient and sender information in the tabs provided. Include **mailing instructions** (select Personal) and add two **cc** recipients.
	❷	Once created, enter a generic letter welcoming the recipient to your company.
	❸	Create an envelope to accompany the letter. Do not include a return address.
	❹	Save the file as a template.
	❺	Create a new file based on your template. Change the background color of the page and then modify the recipient's information.

Appendices

- **Cursor Movement Keys**
- **Shortcut Keys**

APPENDIX A: CURSOR MOVEMENT KEYS

KEYS:	ACTION:
CTRL + ←	Moves to beginning of previous word
CTRL + →	Moves to beginning of next word
END	End of current line
HOME	Beginning of current line
CTRL + ↑	Beginning of previous paragraph
CTRL + ↓	Beginning of next paragraph
CTRL + G	Goes to page number you specify
PG↑	Previous windowful
PG↓	Next windowful
CTRL + HOME	Goes to beginning of document
CTRL + END	Goes to end of document

APPENDIX B: SHORTCUT KEYS

SHORTCUT KEY	ACTION
CTRL + A	Select All
CTRL + B	Bold
CTRL + C	Copy
CTRL + SHIFT + D	Double Underline
CTRL + E	Center
CTRL + SHIFT + F	Font
CTRL + SHIFT + H	Hidden Text
CTRL + I	Italics
CTRL + J	Justify
CTRL + SHIFT + K	Small Caps
CTRL + L	Left Justification
CTRL + M	Indent
CTRL + SHIFT + M	Outdent
CTRL + SHIFT + P	Point Size
CTRL + R	Right Justification
CTRL + U	Underline (Continuous)
CTRL + V	Paste from Clipboard
CTRL + SHIFT + W	Word Underline
CTRL + X	Cut
CTRL + =	Subscript
CTRL + SHIFT + =	Superscript
CTRL + SPACEBAR	Normal Formatting
CTRL + ENTER	Page Break
CTRL + *	Show all non-printing symbols

www.ingramcontent.com/pod-product-compliance
Lightning Source LLC
Chambersburg PA
CBHW060149060326

40690CB00018B/4047